PUEBLO SHIELDS

PUEBLO
SHIELDS

From the Fred Harvey Fine Arts Collection

BY BARTON WRIGHT

NORTHLAND PRESS

Contents

v

THE FRED HARVEY FINE ARTS COLLECTION of some six thousand American Indian and Spanish Colonial articles seeks to preserve the prehistoric and historic art of New Mexico, Arizona and the West.

It is unique in that it was built in the Southwest from 1902 to 1940 under the sponsorship of the Fred Harvey Company and the Harvey Family. When the Fred Harvey Company went public and was later merged into Amfac, Inc., the Fred Harvey Collection became a Foundation. Family members formed the Board along with museum directors.

The Collection was founded for exhibition and demonstration. Today the bulk of the Collection is maintained and exhibited at the Heard Museum in Phoenix, Arizona. Other smaller and more selective portions of the Collection are located in Flagstaff at the Museum of Northern Arizona, and in Santa Fe at the Museum of International Folk Art and the Museum of Navajo Ceremonial Art.

The Pueblo Shields presented in this study are very rare. We offer this and subsequent publications in the hope that the Fred Harvey Fine Arts Collection which was preserved for the future will continue to convey the inspiration of the American Indian and Spanish Colonial artist and craftsman.

BYRON HARVEY
President,
The Fred Harvey
Fine Arts Collection

THE CONCEPT of a defensive, hand-held circular shield is old in the Southwest. This is evidenced by the presence of rock art and mural paintings showing shields, as well as by the survival of prehistoric and historic specimens. In addition to proof of age, mural paintings on excavated kiva walls also depict the different shapes of shields as well as methods of carrying them.

The arrival of the Spanish undoubtedly brought additional shapes and new methods of manufacture to Southwest shields but there was no radical departure from the original native concept. Occasionally Spanish shields were changed to fit native concepts, and Spanish methods of manufacture may have been adopted for the construction of some local shields. When methods of warfare changed with the advent of firearms, the shield did not pass from existence. Rather it continued to be made by the Indians but with greater emphasis placed on its secondary aspect, the ceremonial.

Although it is virtually impossible to assign dates to petroglyphs (rock writing), they do offer a record of sorts and may well illustrate the earliest representations of shields. Their relative ages may be inferred from the superposition of one glyph atop another, as well as from the differential aging of the incised lines. However, the vast majority of shield petroglyphs do not offer this opportunity for relative dating as they usually occur singly. A thorough study of petroglyphs depicting shields or shield-like objects is too broad a field for inclusion here, but a few examples may serve to convey the variety of this pictorial record.

On the Hopi Reservation, there are several very good petroglyphs. Informants for Stephen, an early ethnographer, stated that they were markers for successful battles with unfriendly neighbors. One of the petroglyph shields attributed to the Utes (Stephen: 1936: figure 83) is the double-notched Hispano-Moresque *adarga* of post–fifteenth century invention. This shield (figure 1a) is said to mean that "when the moon was half gone (full moon) with our friends we slew the enemy" (Stephen: 1936: 131). This may well be a reference to the battle between the Utes and the Hopi-Tewa forces sometime in the 1700s, when the Utes were soundly defeated. Another shield petroglyph (figure 1b) is said to commemorate the defeat of a large war party of Apache that attacked Walpi (Stephen: 1936: figure 84). Figure 1c illustrates another shield on the surface of a large boulder near Mishongnovi and a fourth shield at Shipaulovi is shown on figure 1d. Another very distinctive oval petroglyph is attributed by Stephen (1936: 1029) to the Sikyatki people (figure 1e).

At the head of the trail into Havasupai are three painted designs (pictographs) (figure 1g-i) and one petroglyph (figure 1f) which were first noted and described by Lt. John G. Bourke of the United States Cavalry (Bourke: 1884). In view of the Hopi interpretation of their petroglyphs of shields, it would be logical to assume that these also record a victory or possibly several victories by the Havasupai. However, neither the Havasupai nor the Hualapai, their close relatives, used the circular shield. Instead they relied on a folded piece of leather hung from either a bow or short stick, which they held in front of them (Spier: 1928: 250). Therefore, it is probable that these Havasupai rock symbols represent either a different event or a different tribe. In appearance, they are identical with shield designs used by both the Hopi and the Pima (Russell: 1908: figure 46b) (figure 1j). It is the Hopi, however, who have been in closest contact with the Havasupai, having made trading expeditions to them for countless years. The Pima, farther removed geographically, have left little record of contact. Other pictographs of a similar nature have been found at locations such as Betatakin, Kiet Siel (figure 1k) and Canyon de Chelly, Arizona.

One of the best records of early shields comes from mural paintings on the walls of the abandoned Hopi villages of Awatovi and Kawaika-a, recovered by Peabody Museum's Awatovi Expedition. These murals, dated by stylistic changes and pottery types associated with the rooms, were painted between the late fourteenth and early sixteenth centuries. The paintings depict different shapes of shields with varying decorations and methods for carrying. Although the symbolism accompanying the shields is subject to different interpretations there is no doubt that a shield is portrayed. The best example from these murals is the painting of a warrior on the back wall of a room in the

FIGURE I

3

ancient village of Kawaika-a (Smith: 1952: figure 52b). Although the warrior's head has been obliterated, he stands with feet firmly planted and shield on his left arm. He faces an enemy that has obviously been overcome, for the enemy lies on his back with lifeless eyes and an arrow pointed towards his middle. The warrior's shield is decorated with pendent eagle feathers while small dots around the periphery may indicate either decoration or perforations for attachments of additional embellishments. On the front wall of the same room stands another warrior with a shield on his left arm thrust out in front of him toward a second figure aggressively facing him. The shield of this warrior is decorated with whole birds and prayer sticks, although these may be painted symbols rather than actual attachments to the shield. The murals in this room were painted sometime during the fifteenth century (Smith: 1936: 318). Other shield-like elements are common in the mural paintings of both Kawaika-a and Awatovi although most are not as clearly delineated. These elements range from simple white discs associated with figures to elaborate ritual objects.

Prehistoric shields have been excavated from burials at Mesa Verde (Morris-Burgh: 1941), Aztec (Morris: 1924: 193), and Mummy Cave in Canyon del Muerto (Morris-Burgh: *op. cit.* 51). All of these shields are basketry. The coil of the basket is a bundle of three willow rods laced together with yucca in a simple, non-interlocking stitch to form a circular plaque roughly three feet in diameter. The center is bowed outward slightly to leave room for the hand behind the hard wood grip. The shield is supported by this short hand grip, lashed with yucca across the inner convexity. These wooden handles were recovered intact on the Mummy Cave and Aztec specimens which is an extremely rare occurrence. The Mummy Cave shield showed that the positioning of the handle had been changed at least once, possibly for better balance.

The outer surface of the Aztec shield has been painted The central portion is blue-green with a thin rim of red. The outer margin of the shield was covered with pitch and sprinkled with powdered selenite for sparkle (figure 2b). The Mummy Cave shield is also decorated (figure 2a). The central part is covered by a frog-like figure with an orange spot on its back and the rim is painted with a divided border of yellow and blue-gray. This is the same design that occurs as a pictograph on the canyon wall at Betatakin (figure 11). The Mesa Verde shield was badly deteriorated and no longer retained a trace of its decoration; however, it had been constructed in the same fashion

4

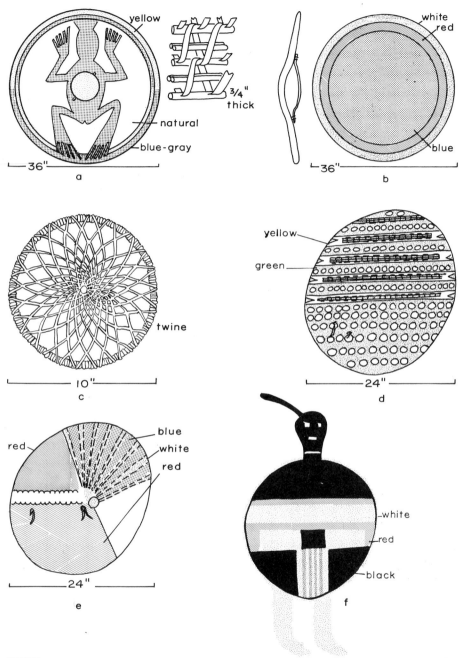

FIGURE 2

5

as the other two examples. These shields are from the Pueblo III period of the Anasazi people dating from A.D. 1100–1300.

It is extremely unlikely that these basketry shields would have deflected or stopped an arrow or a lance. Since lances have never been found in archaeological context in the Southwest, they were probably not a factor in the use of a basketry shield. Native archers, on the other hand, who had little difficulty in penetrating the chain mail of the Spanish (Hotz: 1970: 163) or the padded fiber armor of their *mestizo* warriors, would have had no difficulty in penetrating the half inch of willow rods. Judd believed on the basis of his excavations that arrows, clubs and thrown rocks were the most common implements of warfare in the Southwest (Judd: 1954: 260). It seems logical to assume that basketry shields were used for cushioning the fracturing blows of clubs or thrown rocks rather than defense against arrows.

Judd's observations are supported to some extent by oral traditions among contemporary Indian tribes in the Southwest. Mythologically, for example, the Zuñi fought with bows and arrows, slings, the atl-atl or dart thrower, knives and war clubs. They protected themselves with scorched-hide armor for torso and head and carried a small, circular shield or target. This shield was made of a strong wooden hoop netted across with yucca fiber string and interwoven with cotton (Cushing: 1891: 358, 422). Cushing felt that this was a carrying net adapted to a defensive shield. Whether or not this is true, the event must have taken place far back in antiquity for this same netted shield in miniature accompanied by tiny bows and arrows has been found in caves in an archaeological context. The Zuñi still place these miniatures on war shrines, attached to prayer feathers, for the war gods (Stevenson: 1904: plate XXI). In the Oaqöl, a Hopi woman's dance, two small netted wheels of similar manufacture are used as targets for darts (figure 2c). Beyond myths, little evidence remains other than association of netted wheels with bows and arrows and war shrines to give tenuous support for their use as shields rather than ritual items.

In 1925, three shields were found in a cave along Calf Creek near Torrey, Utah, by Bishop Pectol (Morss: 1931: 69). These shields were of two-ply buffalo hide, nearly two and a half feet in diameter and colorfully painted (see figure 2d,e). Although they were buried by several feet of sand in a small cave, there was no other material with them that might have given a clue to their age. Morss rather hesitantly suggested that they could be of historic age. He based this on their similarity in size to Athapascan ·hi·ld· al-

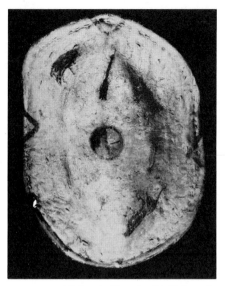

FIGURE 3a. *Old style Navajo shield bought in 1926 from the Hopi House, Fred Harvey Co. at Grand Canyon by Earl Forrest.*

FIGURE 3b. *Modern Navajo shield made by Navajo Johnny in 1962 at Canyon de Chelly, Arizona.*

though the surrounding country abounds with petroglyphs and pictographs of an astounding variety of shields usually attributed to the Fremont Culture. An excellent example of these Fremont shields is shown in David Muench's *Anasazi:* 1974 (see figure 2f). However, the shields of the Apache and Navajo (both Athapascan-speakers) resemble the Plains shields more closely in size than they do those found by Bishop Pectol. The average Navajo shield is about eighteen inches in diameter as compared to the twenty-four inch shield of the Pueblos and Pimas. Morss's identification of these Calf Creek shields as historic is probably correct, not by reason of a size comparable to Athapascan, but more by their resemblance to later Pueblo shields. For although the Pectol shields are more oval, their size and decoration are quite similar to Pueblo bucklers.

In the period just prior to the coming of the Spaniards, there were at least three distinct shield traditions: basketry, netting and hide. Of these three, the basketry and netted shields do not survive into historic times except as miniature ritual objects. Examples of the hide shield have not been found in other than the historic era, though they must predate this period.

The hide shields may be subdivided into sizes and shapes preferred by different groups. The Plains tradition is that of a small round leather shield with a decorated cover that is admirably suited for use on horseback. In general, a Plains shield measured about eighteen inches in diameter and was made of one or two thicknesses of buffalo hide. A secret design, derived from a personal vision, or the vision of a shaman, was painted on its outer surface and was exposed only during war. To preserve the potency of this design, and for ceremonial use, a soft cover was placed over it. This cover was decorated with a related but different design and ornamented with cloth, beads and feathers. Often several covers, one above the other, protected the actual shield. It seems unlikely that this small type of shield predates the arrival of the Spanish and the Indian use of horses.

Specimens of any of these shields are totally lacking, and the records are almost as meager. One example of an early Plains shield used soon after the arrival of the Spanish, but prior to the use of horses by the Indians, may be found on the Segesser II skin painting of the Villasur massacre of 1720. The shields depicted were *adargas* for the Spanish and a large oblong shield for the Pawnee who fought on foot (Hotz: 1970: 98). The scarcity of specimens may in part be due to the Plains practice of destroying a shield at the death of its owner (Mooney: 1901: XXIII). Additionally, the environment of the Plains was not conducive to their preservation.

In the Puebloan world of Arizona and New Mexico, the Plains shield appears to have made little impact. Taos and, to a far lesser extent Zuñi, both have shields that resemble those of the Plains. The Taos shields undoubtedly date from the early 1700s when the Comanche and Kiowa began to attend the summer fair held annually at Taos under Spanish direction (Bancroft: 1889: vol. XVIII: 276–77). The Zuñi shield is probably an import that may have accompanied the introduction of the Comanche social dance. These shields are Plains style in every respect, even to the decorated covers. On the other hand, the Zuñi ceremonial shields such as those belonging to the Priesthood of the Bow (Cushing: 1881: plate X, XI) are larger and resemble the generalized Pueblo form.

Among the migrating Athapascan tribes, a round shield seems to have been the preferred form, although the Navajo occasionally used an elliptical shield. The Franciscan Fathers reported that the small elliptical shield was creased down the middle so that it could be folded (The Franciscan Fathers: 1910: 317). However, the few existing shields constructed in this manner have rigid frames (Underhill: 1953: 119) and could not be folded. It is possible that the Franciscan reference was to the practice of buckling the shield from convex to concave when not in use (Kluckholn: 1971: 368–72). This was done to both the round and the elliptical shields. Hypothetically, the elliptical shield may represent an older form that was superseded by the round type, although it does not in any particular fashion resemble the oval shields found by Bishop Pectol (figure 3a). The round shield of the Navajo was often lashed to a wooden frame, although this depends on the area where the shield was made (see figure 3b). The Apache shield in particular seems far removed from the Plains tradition, for very few were carried, and its purpose seemed to be for supernatural support rather than actual defense (Opler: 1941: 341 and 391). Interestingly enough, it is the Navajo horseman who carried a shield and fought primarily on horseback as did his Spanish and Plains neighbors. Among the Apache, however, only those who fought on foot carried a shield. In this regard, the Apache resemble the Pimas and the Puebloans. In addition, both Navajo and Apache used covers for their shields and did not keep them near their homes.

To the west of the Pueblo area, the Hualapai, Havasupai and Yavapai tribes disdained actual shields although at times they used a buckskin draped over a short stick or over a bow for defense (Kroeber: 1935: 93, and Spier: 1928: 250). The Cocopah to the southwest also scorned the shield as a defensive weapon, but carried one as a banner into battle (Forde: 1931: 173).

Some confusion exists as to whether or not the Pima and Papago had shields or for what length of time. Russell in writing of the Pimas indicated that they had shields as early at 1836. His description of their use in parrying arrows (Russell: 1908: 120) is very reminiscent of Kino's description of Pima fighting techniques (Bolton: 1948: I: 180). The latter suggests the possibility of their use as early as 1698 (Ezell: 1961: 66). Unfortunately, provenience for the two specimens that he illustrated is non-existent, and Pfefferkorn in his encyclopedic listing of "Sonoran" arms did not describe a shield (Treutlien: 1949: 202–4, 211). Consequently, whether the Pima had been users of the Puebloan type shield prior to the Spanish or only in recent times is a point which remains moot. Regardless of when they acquired their shields, they made and used them in a manner more like that of the Puebloans than either the Plains or the Yuman tribes.

As for the tribes immediately to the north of the Puebloans, only the Utes appear to have had shields (Sloan: 1941: 101). The Hopi attribute to them a small shield very similar to the Plains type (Stephen: 1936: 462). It seems reasonable to postulate that since most of their dress, gear and habits were Plains in tradition rather than Southwestern, their shields would be of a Plains nature. The Paiute apparently did not use a shield at all unless some undiscovered report notes this artifact. Their life style and artifacts closely resemble those of their neighbors to the south, the Havasupai and the Hualapai, and it is conceivable that they may have used the leather screen rather than a shield (Powell: 1971: 35–76).

Among the Puebloans, there is little deviation in size or mode of decoration in the existing examples of shields. They preferred a shield larger than their historic neighbors, twenty-four inches in diameter as opposed to eighteen. This generalized shield is similar in shape, decoration and methods of attachment to the prehistoric Pueblo III basketry shields and differs only in size and the material of which it is made. Presumably at some point in the two-hundred-year period between A.D. 1300 and the advent of the Spanish, the Pueblo people shifted from basketry to hides for making a defensive shield. This may, however, be an accident of preservation rather than an actual shift in raw materials. Specific examples of the shields of the various pueblos will be considered later.

The coming of the Spanish to the Southwest brought two new shield types: the *adarga* or bi-lobed shield of thirteenth century Moorish design, and the *rodela* or *escudo,* a small round metal shield. A 1772 list of arms for a Spanish presidio soldier consisted of a broad sword, lance, shield, musket and pistols (Brinkerhoff: 1965: 21). This shield, the *adarga,* accompanied by the lance, was the favored fighting equipment of mounted soldiers until the beginning of the nineteenth century when the introduction of rifles and different methods of warfare brought an end to the use of the *adarga* and lance as well as the *cuerva* or hide armor (*op. cit.*: 89).

The officer's *adarga* was an elaborately decorated shield with the heraldic arms of the king or the owner's family crest, while those of lesser soldiers were ornamented solely with leather stitching in some favored pattern (*op. cit.*: 70). The metal *rodela* never achieved local popularity, undoubtedly due to the scarcity of all metal in the Southwest. However, the hide *rodela* seems to have been the most common form of all, possibly because of the use of native craftsmen by the Spaniards.

Although it may not be possible to support the statement with facts, the inevitable conclusion reached in tracing the history of shields is that the manufacture of small leather shields is a Spanish introduction in the Southwest and part of the horse complex. The distribution of these shields is so closely related to that of horses that the shield rapidly disappears in areas where horses are not used. Secondly, the manufacturing methods for shields vary only slightly among the many tribes making shields.

To make a good shield required the heavy neck or hip hide of a bullock or some equivalent animal such as a horse, buffalo or occasionally an elk. The buffalo hide was the preferred material for shields of the Plains tribes, but for some undetermined reason, the Navajo refused to use the hide of the buffalo for a shield (Kluckholn: 1971: 369). The Mountain Apache used cowhide or horsehide rather than buffalo, but this might represent a difficulty of supply (Goodwin: 1971: 239).

Within each tribe, there appears to have been minor preferences for using one or two thicknesses of leather. The Apache believed that they learned to make their shields from either the Mexicans or the Navajo, but their method of manufacture does not resemble the Navajo. The Apache took a single hide from the middle of the back of a horse or cow and cut out a large square. This square was then pegged to the ground with several inches of clearance. The center of the hide was filled with sand as a weight to stretch and shape it until it dried. After drying, it was trimmed to the desired circular size and a heavy leather loop was then put through the center to the back for a handle. Following the installation of the handle, the front was decorated and a buck-skin bag made to cover it (Goodwin: 1971: 239).

The Navajo method of manufacture was to take the neck or hip hide of a horse or bull as the heaviest leather and cut a circle larger than the desired size of the shield. Then heaping up earth to about the size of an anthill, they heated the earthen hill and put the wet hide over it, weighting it until it dried. If two hides were used, one was cut slightly smaller than the other and both were trimmed to size and then lashed together along the periphery. When using the single hide, the shield was trimmed to actual size after dry-ing; otherwise it was trimmed before drying and the holes for support burned through (Kluckholn: 1971: 369–71).

Among the Puebloans, the manufacturing method was very similar except that the drying was usually done in a pit shaped in the desired form of the shield. The Spaniards consistently used two or more hides for their shields and used the stitching that joined them as a decoration. The Puebloans, on the other hand, who used more than one piece of hide, sewed concentric circles of hidden stitches to attach the two sheets of leather, and then painted a decoration on the front of their shields.

For the Indian, the painting on the shield was often more important than the actual physical protection it afforded. The decoration was a magical device that was used to blind and confuse an enemy in battle or to defeat him by countering his magic (Russell: 1908: 120). An Apache describing a good shield user during a war dance stated:

> He held his shield out in front of him with his left hand, and in his other hand he held a spear. He did well and pretended to be in battle. You couldn't see him at all behind the shield. It was as if he was invisible. Only you could see the shield there.
>
> (Goodwin: 1971: 242)

The Pima fought in a similar fashion holding the shield out at full arm's length and twisting it rapidly as he leaped about. Seen from in front, the shield presented a difficult target and a distraction to enemy bowmen (Woodward: 1933: 166).

In other instances, the shield was believed to impart immunity from harm or to provide supernatural assistance to the carrier. The latter attribute is the most consistently held belief, and because of this supernatural potency, the shields were kept covered lest this power leak away. Both the Navajo and the Apache followed the tradition of the Southern Plains Indians by having a shaman make their shields, imbue them with his supernatural protection and then cover them with buckskin. Only those who had a strong personal power or who could afford the expense of a shaman carried a shield (Opler: 1941: 391–92). The Puebloans, on the other hand, appear to have made and decorated their own shields without the aid of a religious practitioner.

The designs used by each tribe for their shields are distinctive, but usually follow a generalized group tradition. The Navajo tended to paint their shields black or use pictures of war-related objects such as the bow and arrow or the mountain lion. Other favored designs were the sun and moon, lightning, hands, stars, bear paws or the Big Snake. Each element in some way strengthened the user (Kluckholn: 1971: 370). Similarly, the Apache used animals of prey as symbols of strength or painted representations of the Ga'an (deities) on their shields. The covers of Apache shields are among the most unique, for these are painted with the most simple abstract designs such as a red-rimmed circle or a single rosette centered on the cover or lines in varying colors. One very fine example, in the Museum of the American Indian, collected in 1885 by Edward H. Wales, shows a multiplicity of these designs. The Pima almost exclusively chose forms of quartered designs embellishing these with colored lines to add to their deceptiveness when twirled about during battle. Farther to the north, the Hopi elaborated their shields with representations of war-associated kachinas, snakes, owls and eagles, and rarely stars or some other stylized symbol (Wallis and Titiev: 1945: 523–55). Still further north, the Utes favored abstract designs or conventionalized symbols of stars and moons.

Among the Puebloans the shields of Acoma were extremely plain, favoring a simple geometric insignia on a large field of background color. Jemez and Santa Ana favored a design that divided the shield in half horizontally with horned elements above and rays below. In fact, this form of dividing the shield in half horizontally characterized most of the Rio Grande Pueblos. Ranking next to it in popularity was the division of the shield into four equal parts to produce a star-shaped figure rather than a quartered design. Both Taos and Zuñi used comparatively simple shield designs such as a central dot on a plain field and then elaborated their cover designs. Santo Domingo shields were at variance with most of their Pueblo neighbors for they were decorated with animals or combinations of animals and geometric designs after the fashion of the Navajo (or perhaps it was the Navajo in the manner of the Santo Domingo). A complicating factor in assigning designs to particular Pueblos or tribes was the extensive interchange of shields under conditions of warfare. If an enemy was killed where it was possible to retrieve his possessions, a good shield would be taken along with his scalp.

In addition to painting their shields, all tribes decorated them with such materials as red cloth or feathers and beads. Each of these items was believed to aid the shield bearer in some fashion. The feathers, for example, might be those of an owl to help him see at night, or crow feathers to confound the enemy. The red cloth, a trade material, arrived late among the Apache, who simply transferred the earlier feather decorations to the top of the cloth (Goodwin: 1971: 239). Regardless of when the red cloth was introduced among the Southwestern Indians, they all placed it on the top margins of their shields, possibly as a symbol of the blood they intended to shed.

In the Southwest the Pueblo shield was carried by a sling that fitted about the neck of the user letting it hang to the level of the left arm. This loop, attached to the upper third of the shield, allowed it to be swung to the back

13

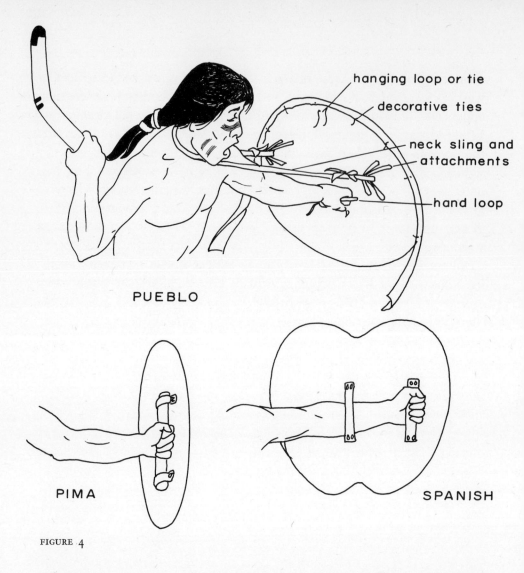

hanging loop or tie

decorative ties

neck sling and
attachments

hand loop

PUEBLO

PIMA

SPANISH

FIGURE 4

when not in use, yet here it was instantly ready should it be needed. The hand-grip was placed in the center of the shield. The Pima-Papago and Navajo used a short wooden handle (figure 4) while the Apache employed a heavy harness leather loop. Spanish shields used a double set of leather straps that held the shield to the forearm and could also be grasped with the left hand for maneuvering. This type of hand grip is much more rigid than the native style, which could be shifted rapidly to cover front or back and still allow use of the warrior's own weapons.

Within the Southwest, disguised by minor variations in manufacture, tribal predilections for decorations, and an almost universal method of attachment, there were three types of shield-users. There was a southern block of warriors who fought on foot and used the shield to blind and confuse their opponents. This included the Pima, the Papago, and the Chiricahua and White Mountain Apaches. A second group of shield-users were those who fought primarily on horseback and utilized smaller shields which were designed to give more supernatural support than physical protection. This style of use is best represented among the Plains Indians and the Navajo. The third group fought primarily on foot and utilized the shield as a true defensive device supplemented by supernatural protection. These were the Puebloan warriors.

In the following discussion of the individual shields represented in the Fred Harvey Fine Arts Collection, virtually all are of Puebloan manufacture or use. Each will be discussed in detail.

PUEBLO SHIELDS

ΛCOMA SHIELD FH 1607 CI Figures 5 and 6

COLLECTED AT ACOMA in 1903, this shield is of two pieces of ¼-inch thick leather held together by five concentric rings of stitching visible on both sides. There are no rips or mends in the shield except for a 1-inch clean cut that goes through both layers of leather to the right of center. There are almost no signs of wear on this shield. A centrally placed thong hand loop is still in place. The strap is very thin (3/16 x 16 inches), knotted at either end for attachment on the front of the shield. The 27-inch adjustable neck sling is attached at either side of the shield to a double loop threaded through four holes in the shield. To make these loops, a 10-inch thong was threaded through each set of four holes and knotted at the back to make a double loop on either side. Along the rim of the shield are two sets of paired holes about one-third of the shield's circumference from each other and 2 inches apart.

FIGURE 5

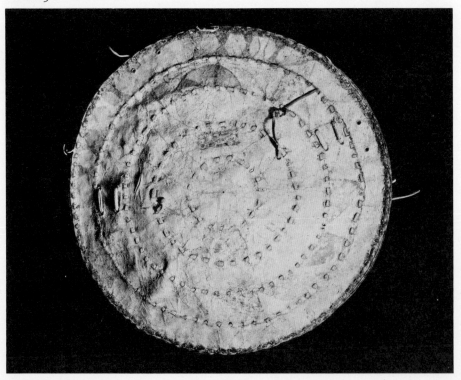

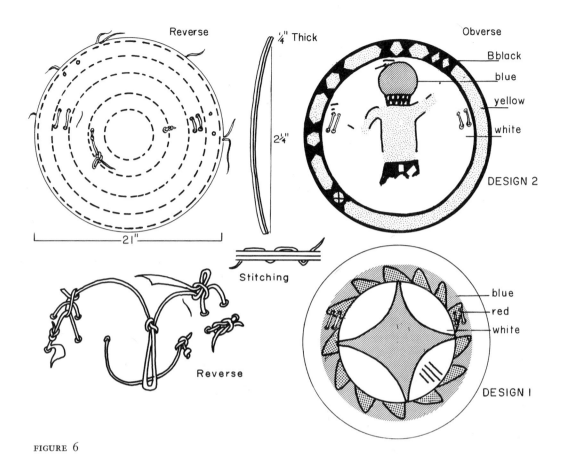

FIGURE 6

These holes may have been used for hanging the shield when not in use, as they are not in the proper position for the attachment of the neck sling. A single small hole in the shield center may be for attachment of a decoration. The shield has two overlapping designs on the exterior. The earlier one is a blue star on a white field with a ring of red and blue triangles surrounding it. Four heavy black lines occupy the lower right field between the points of the star and may represent an even earlier design. Almost covering the star design is a badly eroded figure with a round blue head, yellow torso and black shirt and collar. Half of the rim of this design is painted in lozenge and diamond-shaped segments of yellow on a black background. This last decoration may represent a ceremonial painting of the shield for it differs considerably from other Acoma shield paintings in the collection.

ACOMA SHIELD FH 1610 CI Figures 7 and 8

COLLECTED AT ACOMA in 1905, this shield is a single thickness of hide 22 inches in diameter and ¼ inch thick. The hide was taken from the neck of an animal, probably a bullock, and still shows the striffing at either side and the backbone seam on the rear of the shield. The leather on the facing side of the shield has been either raked or impressed with a series of indentations that follow no set pattern. The appearance is that of corduroy cloth having been pressed into the leather while it was still wet. Three large rips occur in the shield. One tear (3½ x 1½ inches) is triangular, and the other is a slit nearly 2 inches in length near the center of the shield and from the appearance of

FIGURE 7

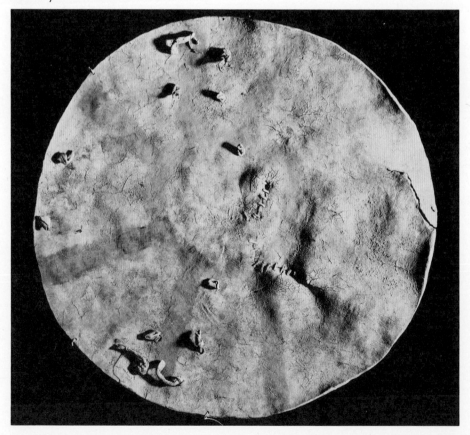

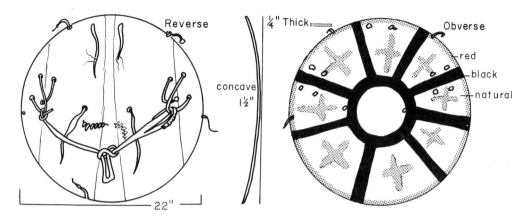

Reverse

concave
1½"

¼" Thick

Obverse

red
black
natural

22"

FIGURE 8

the leather, either could easily have been made by a heavy blow. Both breaks have been mended with either buckskin or leather thongs. A larger tear near the rim is nearly 4 inches in length and has not been mended. This tear gives the appearance of cracking through brittleness and may have occurred during storage. There is almost no sign of wear on the back of the shield with the exception of the edge that would have rubbed against the person carrying it. The hand loop thong is knotted on the front and inserted through the center of the shield. The loop is broken in the middle. A 28-inch neck sling was attached only to the outer loops of a paired set of thongs on either side of the shield and its length could be adjusted only by retying on one side. The hanging loop is on the upper margin of the shield with the ends knotted on the front of the shield to form the loop which has since broken. The broken ends have fragments of sinew stitched through them indicating an effort at repair. Four peripheral ties of red buckskin remain along the rim of the shield. The painted decoration of the shield consists of a central circle with eight radiating lines in dark brown or black on a field of white. Between the spokes or radiating lines are eight red crosses or stars. The rim of the shield is painted red.

ꓘCOMA SHIELD   FH 1611 CI   Figures 9 and 10

COLLECTED AT ACOMA in 1905, this round leather shield is of two thicknesses of hide 23 inches in diameter and each ¼ inch thick. The decorative
stitching is set in seven concentric rings 1½ inches apart with a central cross
attaching the two pieces of leather. This stitching is a leather thong sewed
through a series of parallel cuts in the front and back pieces of leather and
pulled tight. It resembles Spanish leather work. A small amount of wear is
apparent along the things on the rear of the shield. There is no damage to the
shield other than a small tear at the edge that has not been mended and probably is due to storage. A riveted hole is present on the right side halfway

FIGURE 9

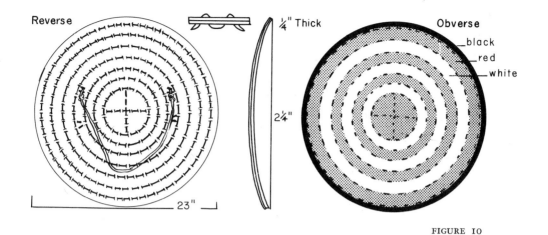

¼" Thick

2¼"

23"

Obverse

black
red
white

FIGURE 10

between the lower strap hole and the margin. The shield is unusual in the lack of holes for the various loops that are normally present on Pueblo shields. There are four areas of attachments each being two slits. The upper pair is used for a sling but it would be impossible to control the shield during battle as it is now rigged. The neck sling was formerly attached to a loop at either side set in 5 inches from the edge and made by inserting the ends of a short strip of leather through both pieces of leather and then knotting the ends on the facing side. At present, these loops are partially gone and only the loop in one set of holes could be used. No hanging loop exists on this shield nor perforations to indicate its locations. Instead the buckskin arm sling has been converted to this purpose. It is quite probable that this shield formerly had a Spanish style hand grip. Peripheral ties for the attachment of the decorative cloth edge are present. Decoration of the shield is a series of red and white alternating rings starting with a red center and ending with a black edging.

ACOMA SHIELD   FH 1614 CI   Figures 11 and 12

COLLECTED IN 1905 at Acoma, this shield is a double thickness of leather ⅜ inch thick and 21½ inches in diameter. The two sheets of leather are attached to each other by four concentric rings of blind stitching. Blind or hidden stitching consists of catching the back side of the facing leather and the front side of the backing leather without penetrating to the surface of either sheet. All four rings are sewn and then progressively pulled tighter until the two sheets of leather are snugged together. The rim of the shield is then saddle stitched to complete the attachment. Both the back and the front of this shield

FIGURE 11

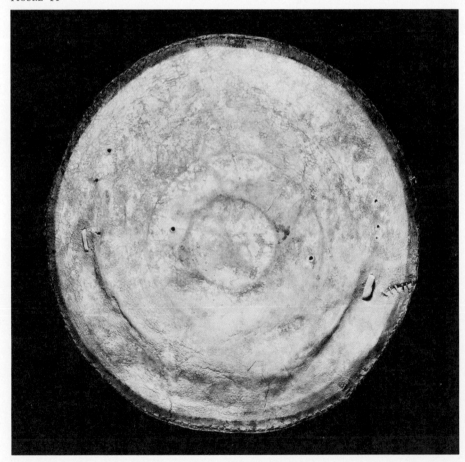

24

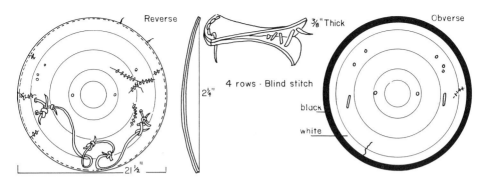

FIGURE 12

show rather extensive wear marks on all high surfaces. Eight rips are present in this shield but only three of them are on the facing leather. All but one has been mended, and one has been mended twice. The backing leather has a large triangular rip and a long tear near one loop attachment that do not penetrate the facing leather and may represent a loop pulling out and being relocated. It is difficult to account for the breakage on the backing sheet and not on the front hide. It is not feasible to join two sheets of leather with blind stitching after they have dried and been fire hardened as might have been the case if an old shield was covered with a new facing. Holes 7½ inches apart in the central portion of the shield indicate the presence of a hand loop. The 24-inch adjustable sling was attached near either edge by a single loop. These single loops were made by passing a thong of leather through one hole across the facing leather and back to form a stitch on the front of the shield. The loop ends were then tied at the back of the shield. An additional set of holes occupying the same position but on the opposite hemisphere of the shield are not in use and probably represent earlier use, for one of the holes is in the large triangular tear. No hanging ties for the shield are present. The peripheral ties for the attachment of the cloth edge are almost completely worn away. Decoration for the shield consists of an all-white ground with a thin (1 inch) rim of black. There is no evidence that this shield has been repainted.

ꓞꓛOMA SHIELD   FH 1618 CI   Figures 13 and 14

COLLECTED AT ACOMA in 1905, this shield is made of a single ¼-inch thickness of hide 22¼ inches in diameter. The leather was taken from the animal's neck where it joins the shoulder. The seam line along the backbone and the striffing is still apparent on both sides of the shield. There is a major tear near the center of the shield that is 2½ inches in length and has been repaired by placing a strip of leather along the tear on the facing side and then sewing across the strip. Three other holes occur in the shield, all of the same shape and dimensions (⅜ inch long) and appear to have been made by perforation

FIGURE 13

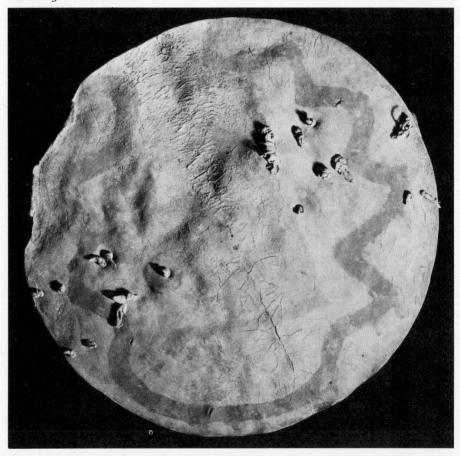

26

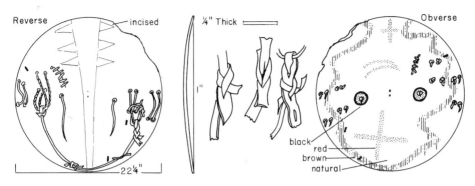

FIGURE 14

from front to back. No attempt has been made to mend these holes. Two small holes are in the center and may represent recent attempts to suspend the shield or may be decorative tie holes. The leather of the shield is quite heavy on one side but thins from ¼ inch to a feather edge on the opposite side where the leather has eroded from its circular shape. A central hand loop with an 8-inch opening was used to control the shield although the loop is now broken. The 24-inch adjustable neck sling is made of a ½-inch buckskin strap, supported at either end by two loops placed a short way in from the rim. These loops are independently knotted on the front side of the shield. From the back, the left hand loops are made of two-strand twisted buckskin. A variant feature of this shield is the presence of four additional loops, two at either side, placed along the horizontal equator of the shield. The outer loop is within ½ inch of the rim of the shield. It is possible that this shield had been cut down from a slightly larger size necessitating the replacement of the neck loop. Decoration of the shield consists of an irregular dark (possibly oily) zigzag line from the top of the shield roughly paralleling the rim around the circumference and ending at the rim a few inches from its beginning. Within these lines at the top of the shield is a single red cross or star. At the bottom is a larger cross or star. Around the knotted ends of the hand loop are red circles rimmed in black that are two inches in diameter. There is a faint indication that the ground of the shield may originally have been yellow. On the rear of this shield is an incised decoration of six triangles placed along the leather seam near the upper portion. The snake motif on the front and the inside decoration are far more common among the Apache (Goodwin: 1971: 242) than at Acoma, and it is interesting to speculate on the possibility of this being a captured shield.

ACOMA SHIELD   FH 1620 CI   Figures 15 and 16

COLLECTED IN 1905 at Acoma, this round shield is made of two thicknesses of leather ¼ inch thick and 22½ inches in diameter. The two leather sheets are held together by seven concentric rings 1½ inches apart with a central cross of leather stitching. A leather thong was inserted through the parallel cuts in the backing and facing leather in such a manner as to make a decorative pattern of stitches similar to Spanish manufacture. Three large cuts or tears and two smaller ones that do not extend through the backing leather of the shield have been mended with simple over and under leather lacing. A

FIGURE 15

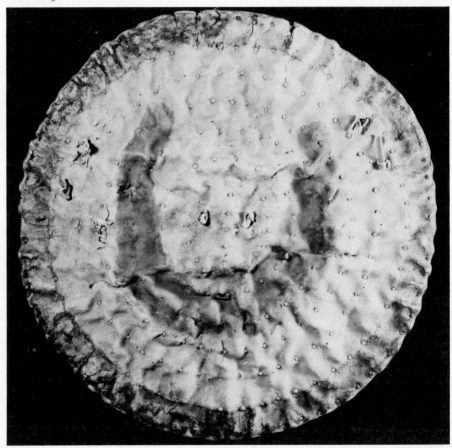

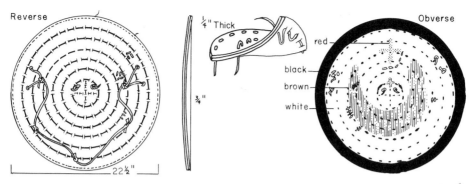

¼" Thick

red

black

brown

white

Obverse

¾"

22½"

FIGURE 16

slight amount of wear shows in places on the back surface. The entire shield is badly distorted, presumably from prolonged exposure to weather. The shield was held by a centrally attached strap of which only the two knotted ends remain. The neck sling was attached 2½ inches in from either edge and slightly above the mid-line of the shield. Attachments were made by inserting both ends of a short length of leather through the shield and then knotting the ends. A single 3-foot-long adjustable strap connected the two short loops. Fragments of peripheral ties for the attachment of a decorative cloth edging are present as well as a ring of thirteen small holes 3½ inches in from the rim. The ground color of the shield is white with a 2-inch black margin. A large red star or cross lies between the horns of a brown crescent moon in the center of the shield. Below the larger star or cross lies a smaller red star. The crescent moon appears to have either been added at a later date or intensified with the addition of an oily substance.

ACOMA SHIELD FH 1621 CI Figures 17 and 18

THIS SHIELD WAS COLLECTED in Acoma in 1906; however, it does not resemble the other Acoman shields. This shield is only 16½ inches in diameter but it is nearly ⅜ inches thick and was undoubtedly made of a buffalo hide, although a bull hide is often this thick. The rim of the shield has been beaten back until a rolled edge has been made. The center of the shield has three perforations made prior to the first painting of the shield. Two are slits ½ inch wide and one is a round hole. All perforated the shield from the front to the back. The perforating objects were then removed from the front of the shield. There is a single small perforation in the middle of the shield

FIGURE 17

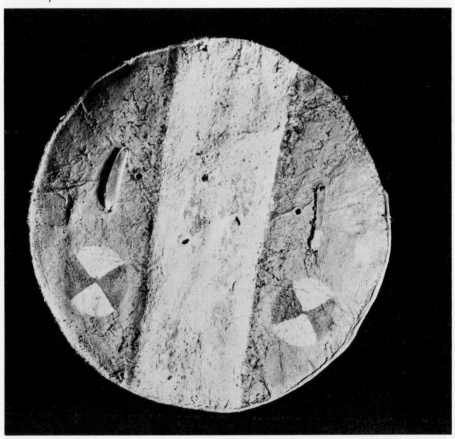

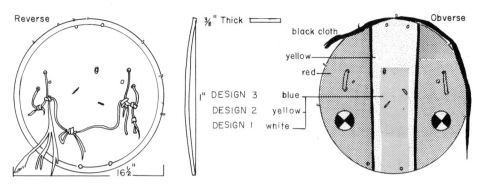

FIGURE 18

that may either have been for attachment of a decoration or a nail hole. The
rear of the shield has an incised line that parallels the entire rim of the shield
½ inch from the margin. There is no hand loop on the shield at present, but
it appears to have been held by a thong across the center of the shield with the
loop ends about 7 inches apart. The neck sling, 38 inches in length, was adjustable but has broken at one end. The ends are attached to single side loops.
Two other sets of holes are placed on the rim of the shield at right angles to
those with the neck sling attached. These paired holes may represent the
attachments of an earlier or larger shield or possibly the presence of a wooden
handle. The decoration of the shield consists at present of a single field of
yellow along the vertical axis of the shield. This is bordered with black which
separates a red field on either side. Within the red lies a circle just below the
loop attachments for the arm sling. These circles are quartered with opposing
colors, black alternating with yellow. The lower two-thirds of the central
field of yellow is filled with a blue rectangle. It is apparent that the central
panel has been painted at least four times. The initial color was all white then
all yellow. Both colors fill the central perforations in the shield. The third
painting was a blue-green rectangle in the lower part of the panel. This was
finally repainted with a much greener paint that is still present. It does not
appear that the outer panels and symbols were ever repainted. A small strip
of black cloth remains attached to the upper margin of the shield. The general appearance and construction of this shield resembles a Plains shield more
than those of Acoma or the other Pueblo groups. It may possibly be a traded
or captured shield incorporated into Acoma.

COMANCHE SHIELD WITH TWO COVERS

FH 258 CI   Figures 19, 20, 21 and 22

THIS PARTICULAR SHIELD is well authenticated. It was purchased in 1904 by a Mr. Huckel of the Fred Harvey Company from Mr. C. R. Massey. It was then sent to Dr. Mooney of the Smithsonian Institution for identification. He in turn sent it to Dr. G. A. Dorsey of the Field Museum in Chicago. The note accompanying the shield reads — "Comanche shield formerly the property of C. R. Massey, Mt. View, Oklahoma." Apparently the shield was shown to Quana, the head chief of the Comanche, but he could not identify it although both covers are new. The shield is small, 17½ inches in diameter but ¼ inch thick, a very heavy hide with the neck striffing still present. The only sign of working is the rounded edge of the shield. There is a center hand grip of two strips of buckskin knotted on the front of the shield and passed through to the rear. The left hand strip is 33 inches long and the right hand thong is 22 inches in length. It is possible that the two thongs were knotted to form the loop, or they may have been grasped loose in one hand. The neck sling is made of knitted cloth of a polychrome color that gives the general impression of a Mexican serape, although it is not. It is attached through three holes at either side of the shield by a thong that passes from the rear of the shield to the front, back to the rear, to the front and again to the rear and is then knotted to form a double loop. The knitted cloth strap (4 inches wide) is tied at either side around these loops with a very short span between them and a loose end hanging nearly 30 inches in length at either side of the shield. In addition (to the foregoing) there is a long strip of horse's mane and tail (30 inches in length) that hangs at either side of the shield and is attached to the same loops. A hanging loop on the upper margin consists of two holes 3½ inches apart but no loop remains. The strap has instead been transferred to the outermost cover. The back side of the shield has a shiny yellowish appearance that may not be paint, but the natural color of the hide. The front side of the shield is whitish with a slightly fuzzy appearance as though it had been scraped. The first cover of the shield is the most ornate of the two covers. It is a very thin well-worked buckskin 4 inches greater in diameter than the shield it covers and held over the shield by a drawstring inserted through numerous parallel slits around the radius of the cover. The front of the cover has a blue circle in the center of the shield from which is suspended a number of short

FIGURE 19

FIGURE 20

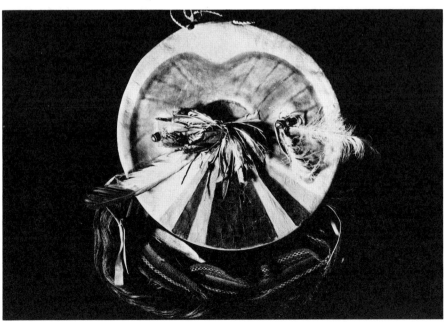

FIGURE 21

($1\frac{1}{4}$ inches) buckskin thongs. Attached to the end of the thongs are flicker tail feathers, bound with sinew to let them flutter freely. Surrounding the flicker feathers is a blue circle with alternating red and blue triangles around its circumference in the manner of sun rays. The field surrounding this is a soft yellow with two elements on the left and one on the right. Immediately next to the central circle on the left is a short red and blue bar set vertically (5/16 inch wide by two inches long). From the center of these two bars, an eagle breast feather is attached. The farthest left hand element is a 2-inch five-pointed star. In the center of the star is a small plain leather circle with a hole. On the right hand side of the shield is a similar device except that the star is six-pointed, and from the center of the circle in the star is suspended a small brass sleigh bell. Directly below the central circle are a series of radiating rays; beginning on the far left is a thin wavy blue line that reaches from the outer points of the radiating triangles to the edge of the shield. This is followed by a thin red line of the same length, then a broad red stripe. Following a very narrow separation is a thinner blue stripe, another separation and then a broad red stripe with a single indigo dot ($\frac{1}{2}$ inch) set an inch from the margin of the shield. Another narrow separation and a very broad blue area and then the left hand sequence is repeated with the exception of the fine wavy lines. The rim of the upper half of the cover is a rainbow of fine lines placed concentrically, beginning with red, then green, indigo, yellow and finally a wider blue stripe. Into the outer blue stripe, sewn with buckskin, are two pieces of indigo stroud with white ends. The upper ends do not quite meet at the top of the shield, and the lower ends hang 34 inches below the shield. From these two strips hang eagle tail feathers; nine on the left and seven on the right. These feathers are attached to the cloth by the simple expedient of cutting away half the quill for a short distance, sharpening the remaining portion and inserting it through the margin of the cloth and then looping it back and into the quill base. This allows the eagle feathers to flutter freely. The majority of the feathers on this shield are partially immature and are flecked with black. The outer cover is in essence an abbreviated form of the main cover. The diameter is 6 inches greater than the shield, the attachment with the drawstring is the same, but the buckskin of the cover is thicker. At the top of this cover is a twisted buckskin thong tied through two holes $3\frac{1}{2}$ inches apart. The loop is 20 inches long and the loose ends hang 6 inches. From the center of the cover tied to buckskin thongs is a very large bunch of flicker wing feathers and one eagle tail feather. The flicker feathers appear to

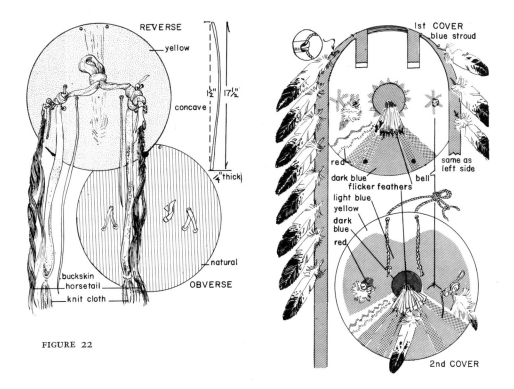

FIGURE 22

be from both yellow- and red-shafted flickers. Surrounding this feather knot is a large indigo spot 4½ inches in diameter. This is set in a bi-lobed lighter blue field with erratically radiating darker blue lines that occupies the top two-thirds of the shield and is surrounded by yellow. On the left-hand side of the shield is a doublet of a red and blue bar from the center of which is suspended two brass sleigh bells and an eagle breast feather. In a similar position on the right hand side is an eagle feather with two brass sleigh bells. The lower portion of the shield appears to be a repetition of the inner shield except that the two dark indigo spots are missing. In addition, the color of the wavy lines has been reversed, and they are painted on the natural color of the buckskin.

ZUNI SHIELD WITH DOUBLE COVER

FH 1595   Figures 23, 24, 25 and 26

IT IS UNKNOWN at what time this particular shield was purchased from the Zuñi or even that it was purchased there. Although it is attributed to them it resembles a Plains shield in every way. The shield is a single thickness of hide (⅜ inch) and the diameter (18½ inches) is quite small compared to most Pueblo shields. It has the appearance of having been trimmed around the edges to lessen the diameter of the shield, for two holes on the upper margin of the shield have been sliced in half. The shield is atypical in another respect, as there was apparently no hand grip. Across the horizontal axis of

FIGURE 23

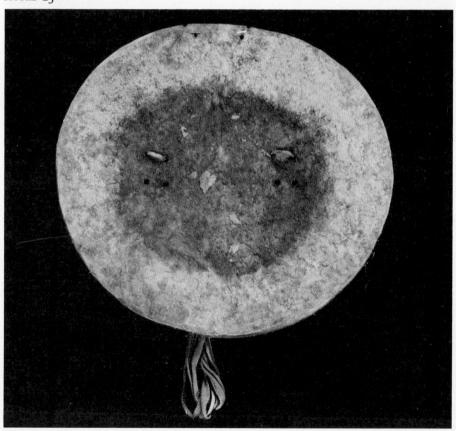

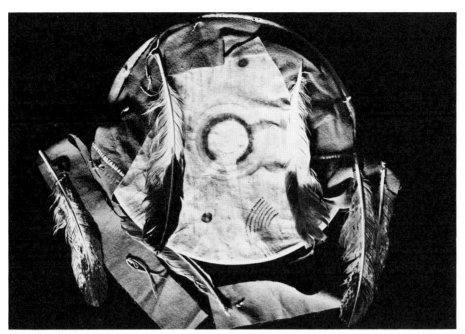

FIGURE 24

the shield are two sets of four holes, one on either side of center. The upper two holes at either side have had a strip of rawhide inserted through them and knotted on the back, and to these loops (5½ inches apart) has been tied a wide band of multi-colored, knitted cloth. A loose knot pulls the center of the cloth up so that it does not hang and either end is tightly held with a square knot to the loop. The knitted cloth is woven in a chain stitch that un- ravels easily but appears to have a finished margin as it ravels. There are two sets of holes along the upper margin of the shield that may have been used for hanging holes. The outer set (3½ inches apart) has been cut in two, but the lower set (2½ inches apart) may have had a hanging loop although no por- tion of the thong remains. Decoration on the front of the shield is quite sim- ple and is limited to a reddish brown spot in the center surrounded by a greenish band. The remainder of the shield is natural. The inner cover of shield is quite intricately decorated in the manner of a Plains shield. The cover is of buckskin with a diameter greater than the shield that it covers. The margin has been turned back approximately 5½ inches and the outer 1½- inch slit at right angles to the edge and a drawstring inserted through the slits. Around the upper two-thirds of the margin of the shield cover, a strip of stroud or American Flannel has been sewn with very fine cobbler's twine. At the horizontal axis of the cover, the cloth at either side has been lapped and stitched together and across the joint a thin band of yellow cloth has been sewed to cover the joint. From this point downward, the two strips are allowed to hang free 3 inches wide and 40 inches long. Three eagle feathers were attached to either side of the straight hanging pieces of cloth; and two along the curved upper portion of the shield cover. These feathers are attached by buskskin and cloth to the red strip. The usual manner seems to have been to insert a strip of buckskin up the hollow quill of the feather, then notch the quill about 1 inch from the end and bring the thong out and either knot it or tie it back on itself. Some of the feathers have the thong simply knotted around the shaft or quill, but this is probably to keep the feather with the shield and was done at a much later date. Decoration of the first cover

FIGURE 25

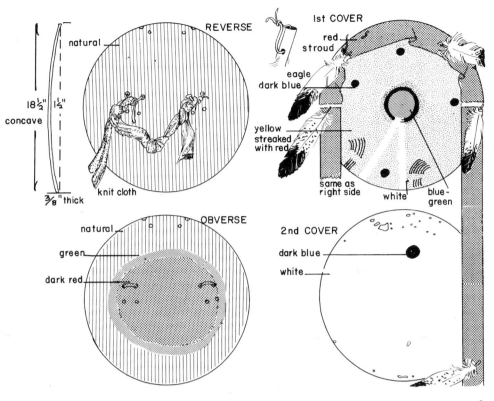

FIGURE 26

consists of a field of yellow, mottled with vertical stripes of red that have a roughly squarish shape as though a square-ended stick had been dipped into red paint, pressed against the cover and stroked downward till the paint wore off. The center of the shield cover is a gray-white circle that at one time was painted a turquoise blue and surrounding it are concentric rings of color in this order; black, red, light yellow, and dark yellow. From the bottom of this spot are two lines of white to the lower margin of the cover and cutting across the concentric rings. Between the two lines is a large black spot, three others lie to the right, left and directly above the central spot. At either side of the lines of white are a series of seven curved black lines above four short straight lines. The second cover of the shield (figure 25) is absolutely plain with an overlap of 3 inches and a slightly mottled appearance as though at one time white had covered the cover and has now worn off. The cover is extremely old and in the upper half is a dark spot that may or may not have been a part of the decoration. Several holes have worn through the very thin cover.

SANTO DOMINGO SHIELD

FH 1617 CI   Figures 27 and 28

NO PURCHASE DATE exists for this shield, but it would appear to have been purchased at relatively the same time that the other shields of the collection were acquired. The shield, 19 inches in diameter, is made of two sheets of leather ¼ inch thick sewed together by seven concentric rings of blind stitching. The outer edge of the shield has a rough-cut appearance with holes at the extreme edge and a type of sewing with sinew thread that is not consistent

FIGURE 27

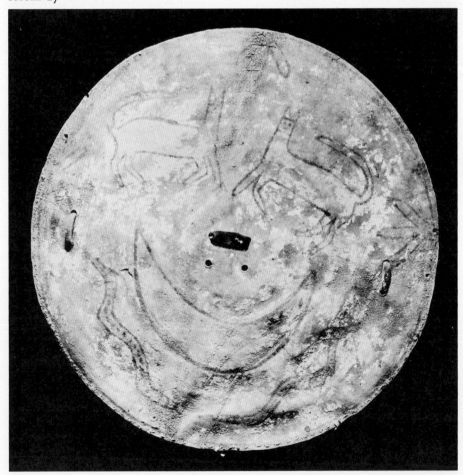

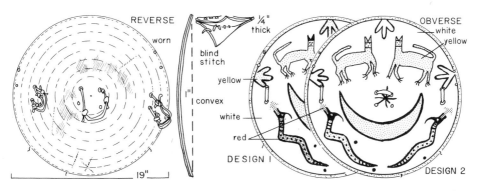

FIGURE 28

with the stitching on the remainder of the shield. There are areas of very heavy wear in the center where the hand and forearm would rub. The 5-inch-wide hand loop passes through the upper set of four holes that occupies the central portion of the shield. These four holes probably represent two different settings for the hand loop. There is also along the horizontal axis of the shield a double set of holes for the neck sling which is missing although the loops are present. There are two other pairs of holes on either side far above those that are presently used for attachment, at the margin of the shield. Seemingly the shield has been cut down from a larger one at some point for one of these holes is cut in half by the rim. A central decorative tie hole is present, but somewhat larger than usual. The design of the shield has been painted over at least once, but the actual sequence of painting is quite difficult to interpret. The first design appears to have been almost exactly the same as the last design. In the upper half of the shield at right, left and top along the rim of the shield are three yellow bird tracks outlined in black. Directly under the top central one are two mountain lions with claws extended and tails arched over their backs. In the lower half of the shield is a single half moon in yellow outlined in black on a white field. At either side, a water serpent with a red tongue and black head and red body is located. The entire outer rim of the shield is a double band of black with an outer ring of yellow. In the center of the shield is a line drawing of an eight-pointed star. It is possible that there was a second design which was white over the entire shield as the white paint both underlies the yellow of the last design and overlies portions of the older designs such as the bird tracks and the ears of the mountain lions. The final design includes the dropping of the bird tracks, the central star and the changing of the water serpents from red to yellow.

41

ZIA SHIELD FH 1615 CI Figures 29 and 30

PURCHASED IN ZIA prior to 1906, this shield is 23 inches in diameter and is made of a single sheet of leather 5/32 inch thick. The leather of the shield is cracked and brittle with age or misuse. A crack along the vertical axis of the shield has been carefully mended, but the lower portions of the mending thong have also been worn away. Scattered across the left and lower portions of the shield on the back side are a series of perforations or slits that resemble penetrations by projectile points. These, in most cases, are not evident on the front side of the shield possibly indicating that the shield may have been reversed. No hang thong remains on the shield, although the two attachment

FIGURE 29

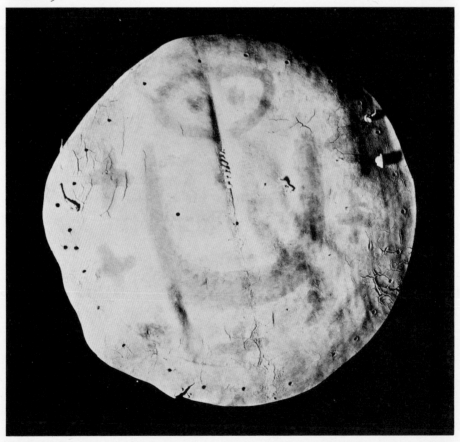

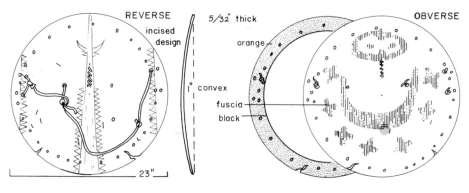

FIGURE 30

holes lie along the horizontal axis 8 inches apart. The neck sling was knotted
on the front of the shield using two sets of paired holes at either side of the
shield. The total length of the neck sling is 36 inches. Set along the periphery
of the shield are a number of fairly large holes that were probably used for
additional decoration, although no evidence remains of the type of decoration. It is possible that some of these may have been used for the hanging loop.
The back of the shield is decorated with an incised pattern that utilized the
natural divisions of the neck hide. At either side of the neck ridge, a line of
serrations has been incised topped by a crescent moon. At either side of the
shield, an additional vertical line of serrations has been added. The decorations on the face of the shield belong to two different periods. The first design
appears to have been a single orange band, 2½ inches wide, around the rim of
the shield and a 1 inch diameter spot in the lower half of the shield along the
vertical axis. The second design seems to have been added quite recently and
is a series of figures done in a rather violent fuchsia color, apparently a dye of
some sort. This design is a stylized owl head at the top of the shield overlying
what appears to be a crescent moon or could be a stylized owl body. Around
this element are placed seven stars or crosses which lie between the older
border and the recent crescent.

ISLETA SHIELD FH 1599 CI Figures 31, 32 and 33

PURCHASED IN ISLETA prior to 1910, this shield is 24½ inches in diameter. It is made of a single thickness of leather, ¼ inch, taken from the hip area of the animal and protected by a single thin buckskin cover. The central hand loop had a width of 6 inches with a single thong remaining. The neck sling attachment is two separate loops with the connecting thong missing. These loops were constructed by using four holes on either side of the shield and knotting the thongs on the front of the shield. The hanging loop was

FIGURE 31

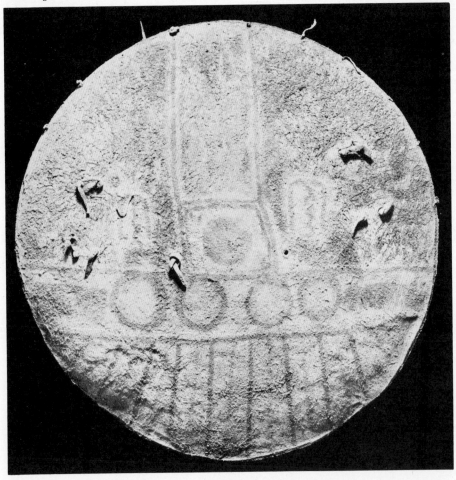

FIGURE 32

placed at the extreme upper margin of the shield. Peripheral buckskin ties are present around the entire upper half of the shield where they were stitched through the leather and knotted. Decoration of the shield consists of a band across the horizontal axis of the shield with four circles in it and a block at either rim. Dependent from the band are a series of alternating rays of natural yellowish leather, the white field color and red stripes. Above the band, along the vertical axis, is a single red spot within a square of natural leather, yellow and then red banding. This square is connected to the upper rim by two red lines. At either side, an upside-down U with a zigzag pendent from its center is done in red on a white patch. The remainder of the upper half of the shield is a dark blue-gray. The cover for this shield is of very thin pliable buckskin with a drawstring inserted through parallel cuts at the margin. The cover has a fairly simple decoration; at the rim, there is a narrow green band enclosing a yellow field. In the center is a darker yellow circle 4 inches across. This circle is surrounded by concentric rings of green, blue, red and blue.

FIGURE 33

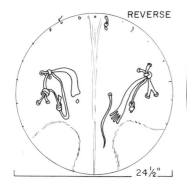
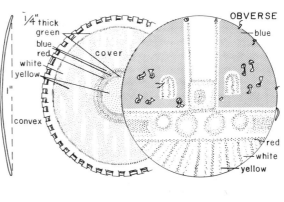

TESUQUE SHIELD FH 1623 CI Figures 34 and 35

THERE IS NO PURCHASE DATE for this shield, but the tag is in the same handwriting as the other shields, and there is no reason not to believe that it was purchased at about the same time. It is a poorly made shield 21 inches in diameter, made of two thicknesses of leather with a combined size of ⅜ inch. These two elements have been whipped together at the edges with a running stitch of buckskin, the outer leather being pulled down over the back piece to make a curled edge. Very thin leather was used for the two pieces,

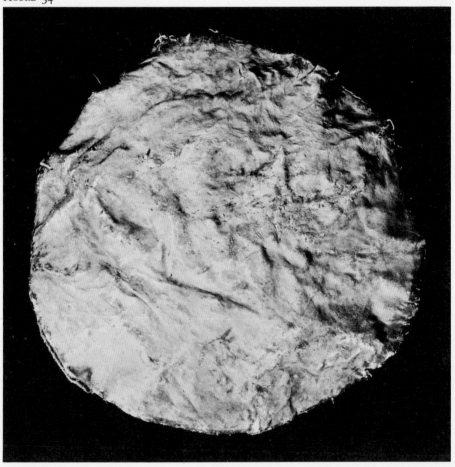

46

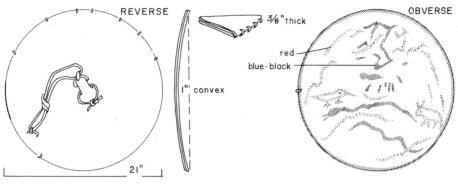

3/8 " thick

red

blue - black

1 " convex

21"

FIGURE 35

and there is evidence to indicate that the membrane was not removed from either piece of leather before manufacture. There is no apparent hanging loop at the rim of the shield. The only attachments seem to be a long and a short loop of buckskin that are fastened to the back piece of leather in the center of the shield. These could not have supported any weight nor much movement without pulling out. There are a few scattered buckskin ties along the periphery of the upper third of the shield. Again, there appear to have been at least two sets of decoration applied to the shield, the older being a set of blue-black lines that apparently represent snakes and a horse (?). Later, the shield was decorated with red paint and a crude bird and animal placed at right angles to the earlier decorations and a red band painted along the rim. Splotches of red occur randomly across the face of the shield and on the straps at the rear. These red splashes of color were most certainly applied after the shield had begun to wrinkle, as the color is quite heavy on the top of the ridges rather than in the depressions. Certainly, this shield was made by an amateur or at least someone who had never seen a shield constructed.

JEMEZ SHIELD   FH 1601 CI   Figures 36 and 37

COLLECTED AT JEMEZ in 1908, this shield is made of a double thickness of leather 24½ inches in diameter and ¼ inch thick. The two pieces of leather have been joined by stitching only around the periphery with a very fine stitch set into a groove. The bottom section of the inner leather is badly cracked and has broken the stitching in one portion of the rim. The hand loop holes in the center of the shield now have the neck sling in this position. Compared with other shields, the insertion of the long strap into the hand loop holes is probably the result of later tampering. Formerly, this shield utilized a four-hole neck support. However, on the right hand side, two addi-

FIGURE 36

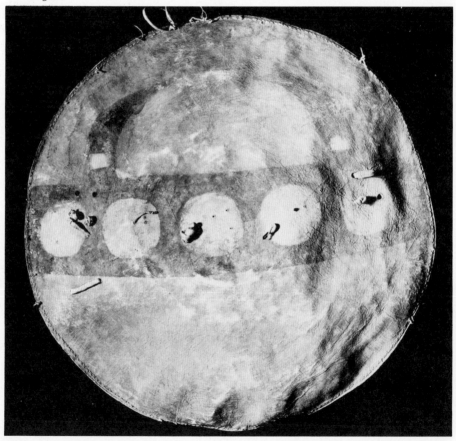

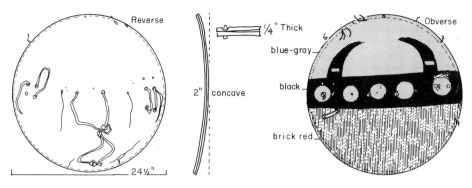

FIGURE 37

tional perforations are placed above the axis of the shield making six holes. Presumably these two holes are an adjustment in the balance for a particular user. A single hole is present on the upper edge of the shield possibly for a hanging loop. Placed slightly above the hand loop ends and to the outside are two very thin strings of buckskin, apparently used for eagle feather ties on the front of the shield. Several other small holes near these and in the center of the shield indicate that there were additional feather ties or the ties had been moved at some time. A few decorative edging ties remain on the periphery of the shield, although almost all of them are broken off close to the shield surface. The decoration of the shield consists of a black band across the horizontal axis of the shield surmounted by two incurving black horns. This band is broken with five circles, and the horns by two rectangular blocks that allow the field color to show through. The field color of the upper half is blue-gray and the bottom a dark brick red.

JEMEZ SHIELD FH 1602 CI Figures 38 and 39

COLLECTED AT JEMEZ in 1915, from the oldest cacique in the village, this shield is composed of two pieces of leather 23 inches in diameter and with a combined thickness of ¼ inch. The leather has been joined at the rim by rather fine stitching set into a slight groove plus three rings of blind stitching. There is no evidence of wear on the shield. The shield is concave, but appears to have been warped into this shape as the bottom edge has a wide tear in the

FIGURE 38

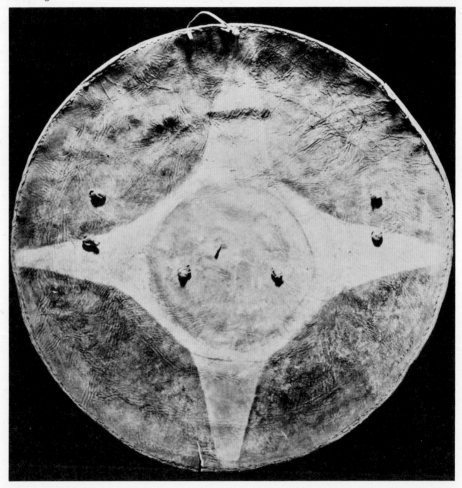

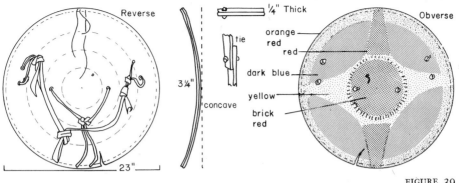

Reverse · ¼" Thick · tie · orange · red · red · dark blue · yellow · brick red · concave · 3¼" · 23" · Obverse

FIGURE 39

leather that has not been mended and appears relatively new. The hand grip loop is still in position and is attached by knotting on the front. The 28-inch neck sling has a two hole attachment and is also fastened by knotting on the front of the shield. The hanging loop at the upper margin consists of two perforations with three strips of buckskin inserted into the left hand hole. A remnant of a tie is present near the center of the shield. Its placement is reversed for the fastening knot is on the front of the shield and the string hung to the rear before being broken off. The decoration of the shield seems to be a combination of a sun symbol in the center of the shield that overlies a simple four-pointed star. The star is done with two opposing arms in yellow and two in red with an orange edging to the shield. The field color is a very dark blue gray. Outlines of all of the designs have been drawn in first with a dark brown line and then filled in with color. There appears to have been no overpainting on this shield.

JEMEZ SHIELD   FH 1604 CI   Figures 40 and 41

COLLECTED IN 1908, this shield is composed of two pieces of leather 22 inches in diameter and with a combined thickness of 5/16 inch. The two pieces of leather have been stitched together around the edge of the shield with a fairly fine cobbler's stitch set into a groove. The shield is concave and split along the bottom margin. In the lower left hand quadrant of the shield is a single slit ⅝ inch wide on the front and only ⅜ inch wide on the rear that appears to have been made by a thin sharp instrument and may represent an arrow penetration. In the same area are three thin stripes of dried blood.

FIGURE 40

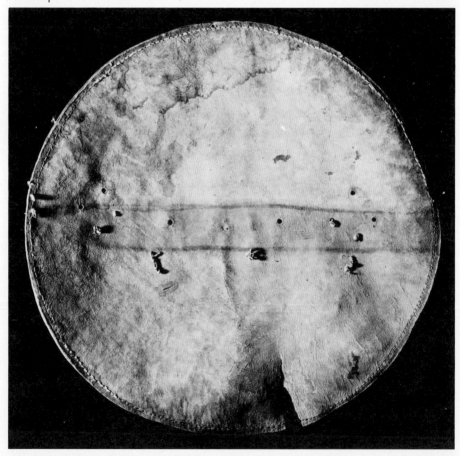

52

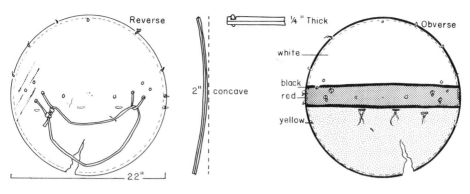

FIGURE 41

The hand grip loop has been lost from the central holes. However, the 30-inch neck sling is still attached through the side loops which are knotted on the shield front. The shield has holes for a hanging loop on the upper margin but a strap is no longer in position. Ties for decorative edging are present along two-thirds of the periphery of the shield. On the left rim of the shield at the horizontal axis are two heavy knots of buckskin for which no apparent purpose can be determined. In addition to the above ties, there are three sets of holes just below the horizontal axis of the shield. Through each of these sets, a length of string has been passed and knotted to hold it in position. Bits of feathers are still present on the string indicating that it was used to suspend feather decorations. The decoration of the shield consists of a central band of red along its horizontal axis. This band is outlined in black as is the rim of the shield. Above this band, the field color is white and below it is a yellow ochre.

JEMEZ SHIELD   FH 1606 CI   Figures 42 and 43

THIS SHIELD WAS COLLECTED in 1906 at Jemez and is composed of a single sheet of leather 21¾ inches in diameter and 3/16 inch thick. Formerly, it was joined to a back sheet with six rings of blind stitching and a rim stitch. The rim stitch has been trimmed away and evidence for it exists in only one portion of the shield. None of the actual blind stitching remains, only the holes to indicate its former attachment. The hand loop is made by passing the strap through to the front of the shield and then to the back and knotting it.

FIGURE 42

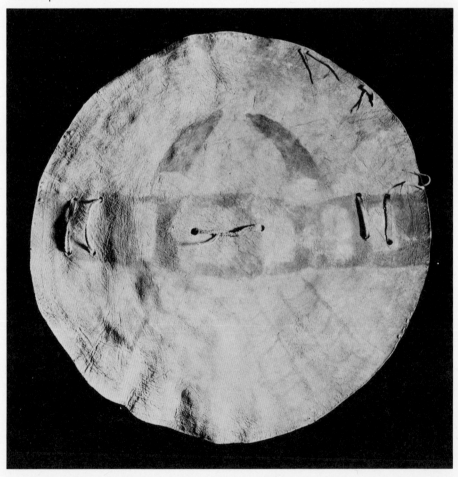

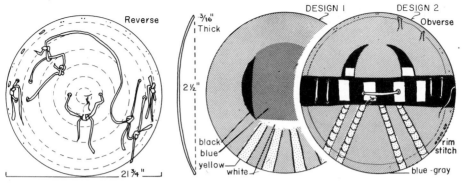

FIGURE 43

The neck sling has a four-hole support and is attached in the same manner as the hand loop. The 22-inch strap has a sliding knot at either end to allow for adjustment. Around the rim of the shield are double holes for the decorative edging ties. A single central feather tie of cotton string remains on the shield. Around the periphery of the shield approximately an inch from the rim is a single incised line on the facing side. This shield has two designs, one over the top of the other. The first design is almost obliterated, but appears to be similar to the later one along the lower margin. The central portion was first a single blue circle with black arcs to the right and left and a white arc at the base of the circle. From the lower margin of this circle, four radiating yellow lines were painted on the blue gray field of the remainder of the shield. The second design is a horizontal band of black across the center of the shield broken by four white rectangles near the center. Above the line are two black incurving horns with a white rectangle in each base which overlie the blue gray field. Four radiating yellow lines are in the lower half of the shield again overlying the blue gray field. Within each yellow band is a series of thin black arcs that give the band the appearance of spider webbing.

JEMEZ SHIELD AND COVER

FH 1609 CI   Figures 44, 45 and 46

PURCHASED IN JEMEZ in 1901, this shield is 21 inches in diameter and composed of two pieces of leather ¼-inch thick enclosed in a well-tanned buckskin cover. The two pieces of leather are held together at the rim by a simple over and under stitch of erratic quality and by seven rings of blind stitching. Four breaks occur on the back side of the shield and all have been mended. The stitching on one of the breaks has been removed or worn through. The entire reverse side shows areas of wear, primarily on the central portion and along most of the higher parts of the shield. On the front of the shield, wear has almost broken through the ridges formed by the blind stitching. A hand loop is in the center of the shield consisting now of two short ends of leather. The 32-inch neck sling has a four-hole attachment with an adjustable right end. No hanging loop is present on the margin of the shield; a single peripheral tie is present along the top margin. Also between the first and second rings of blind stitching from the edge are a series of holes that

FIGURE 44

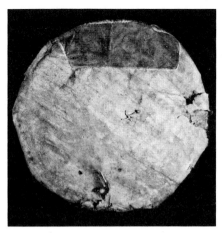

FIGURE 45

encircle the shield. In the exact center is a perforation, and near it are two other small holes. Undoubtedly, all of these were used for the attachment of decorations. The shield was covered with a soft, well-tanned buckskin cover that is very worn and patched. The center has a small buckskin tie probably for the fastening of a feather. It is possible that this shield has been overpainted, but the underlying design is extremely difficult to separate. The periphery of the shield is painted red in a band that shows above the horizontal black band and through the two openings at either end. In the lower half, the red is still there but it appears to have been painted over with a strong yellow. The central opening in the black band is red and this red appears to have once been much larger and reached from the base of the left horn to the base of the right horn in a circle, but again the yellow of the lower half obscures this. The field color lying between the horns, while still the same blue green as that outside of the horns, is several shades darker and the tips of the horns appear to connect with an even darker line. The two outside circles within the central black band appear to have both been white, though at the present, the left-hand circle appears more yellowish.

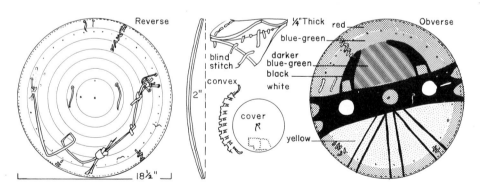

FIGURE 46

JEMEZ SHIELD AND COVER

FH 1612 CI   Figures 47, 48 and 49

COLLECTED AT JEMEZ in 1910, this shield, which is smaller than most, is only 18½ inches in diameter and ¼-inch thick. Two sheets of leather were blind stitched in three concentric rings, and the outer rim joined with a crude cobbler's stitch. This shield has a cover of very soft buckskin. Some breakage of the backing leather has occurred, but this does not reach through to the front of the shield. On the top margin are two small incised triangles cut very shallowly into the leather. To the right of the shield is a single cut into the front leather ⅝ inch long. Two sets of holes exist for the hand loop. Both

FIGURE 47

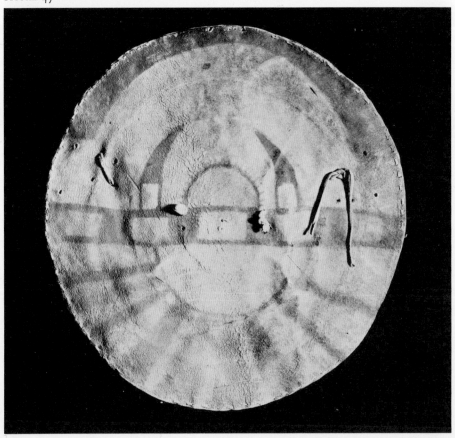

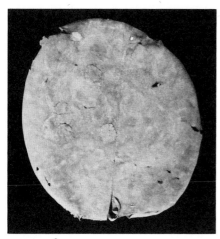

FIGURE 48

are along the horizontal axis of the shield, but only the upper set has a thong. The grip is attached on the front of the shield by knotting. The 32-inch neck sling is secured to a four-hole attachment with the holes having been moved at least once so that there are now six sets of holes. The center and bottom inside hole on the left are used for the thong, and the top inside hole on the right to make a three-hole attachment. The hanging loop position is marked by two holes along the top margin of the shield. The peripheral ties that remain were inserted between the two sheets of leather. There is a central tie hole present, but no tie. The red and yellow on the front of the shield are a much brighter color than could be achieved with native paints. A narrow black band across the shield is broken by five squares: red, blue gray, yellow, blue gray, red. Above it are two incurving black horns with a yellow square in the base of each. Between the horns on the blue gray field color is a hemispherical red sun with short radiating black lines. A black band borders the upper margin. Below the band is a yellow circle edged in black with red lines radiating toward the center. The rays beneath are yellow ochre with black bands on the two sides and black with narrow red lines between. The exterior of the buckskin cover has a soft red tone with rusty brown splotches.

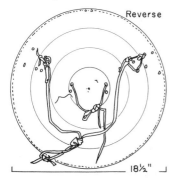

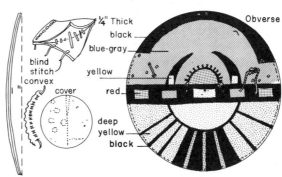

FIGURE 49

59

JEMEZ SHIELD FH 1616 CI Figures 50 and 51

COLLECTED AT JEMEZ in 1908, this shield is 22½ inches in diameter and ¼-inch thick and composed of two sheets of leather. The two pieces of leather are attached by seven rings of blind stitching and very neat cobbler's stitching set into a groove at the rim of the shield. The shield is quite old or well used, for the backing sheet is broken and perforated many times. The shield is concave at present, but this may be due to warping. A central hand loop existed at one time, but the leather has broken out around the holes until it is impossible to determine the exact position. The neck sling appears to have been a

FIGURE 50

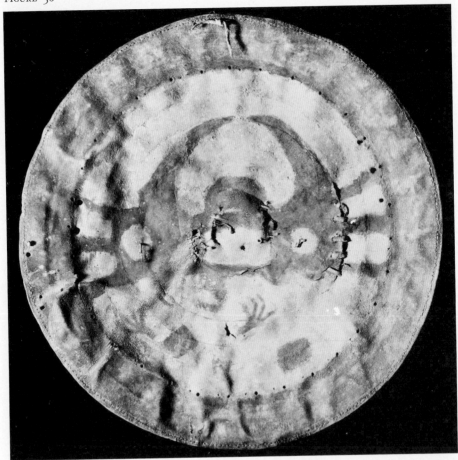

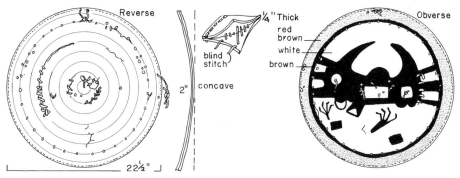

FIGURE 51

two-hole attachment, although no sling remains. A hanging loop exists at the top of the shield, but the buckskin that is inserted in the holes is obviously quite recent. On the right side of the shield at the rim is a set of holes with a single loop of buckskin, but the holes are in the wrong position for a hanging loop. Three very small ties, probably for feathers, are set along the horizontal axis of the shield. Decoration of the shield is in very dull colors. The rim color is a dull brick red and the white field almost a gray. The horned band and the feet are a dull brownish black. Along the horizontal axis of the shield is a black band surmounted by two black incurving horns with a small black hemisphere between. Either end of the band is broken by two gray rectangles lying side by side. Toward the center from these at either side is a gray circle and in the middle a large gray rectangle. Below the band to the left are two brownish four-toed bird or animal feet separated by a black rectangle on a gray field. In the lower right of the same field is a second rectangle. Pendent from the base of the black band are two erratically shaped forms that may represent an earlier design obscured by the gray mud of the later design.

SANTA ANA SHIELD WITH COVER

FH 1603 CI   Figures 52, 53 and 54

THIS SHIELD WAS PURCHASED in Santa Ana in 1908. It is a single ¼-inch thickness of buffalo neck hide with a deep convexity and a diameter of 23½ inches. Two large tears and the beginning of a third along the bottom margin of the shield have been neatly mended by whipping with buckskin. There are two holes in the shield also. From the rear on the left-hand side of the shield is a small hole that has penetrated from front to back pushing fibers of leather to the rear as it emerged. The hole 3/16 inch in diameter appears too small to

FIGURE 52

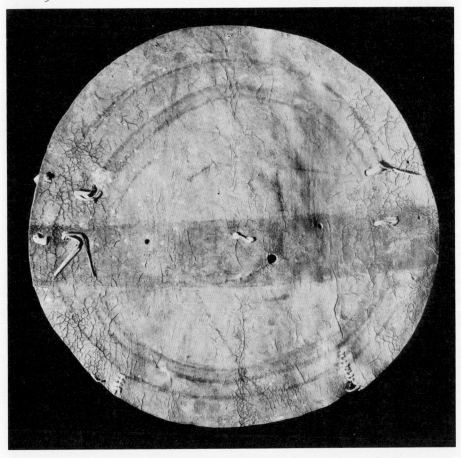

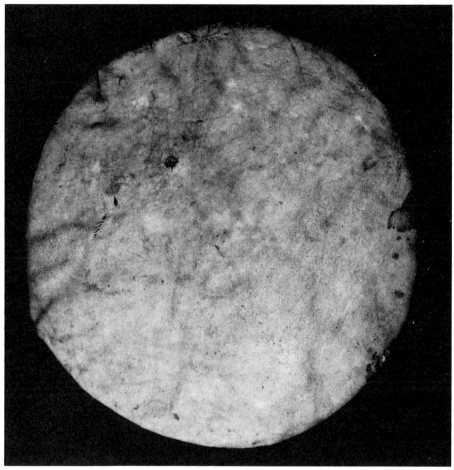

FIGURE 53

be a bullet hole unless it was made by a .22 caliber weapon. Paint from the last design fills the hole on the front side. The second hole is quite large, 7/16 inch, and is just below and left of center. It is indented on the back of the shield but there is no evidence remaining of any extrusion to the front, and it does not show any wear. The hand grip holes along the horizontal axis of the shield are almost 2 inches farther apart than on other shields. The support for the neck sling is a set of four holes at either side; the sling is not present. Both sides of the shield have three sets of paired holes, but only the inner four were used for the sling, and they still retain tag ends of leather. Another pair of holes at the upper margin of the shield probably served for a hanging loop.

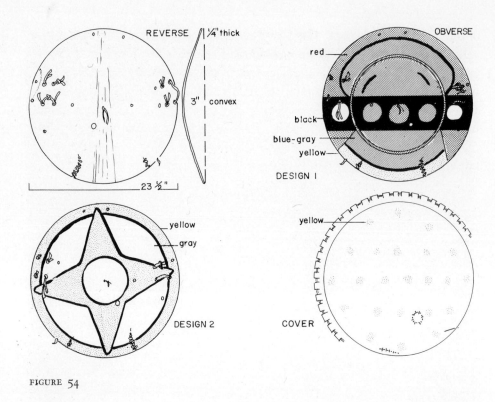

FIGURE 54

No peripheral ties are present, but a small central thong of buckskin is still in place and was undoubtedly used for suspension of a decoration. On the face of the shield, the right-hand loop for the neck sling has a fragment of feather attachment still in place. The quill of the feather was flattened and bent back upon itself and tightly bound with sinew. Through this loop, a piece of buckskin thong was passed and tied to the neck sling where it passed over the face of the shield. The designs on this shield were definitely made at two different times. The first design consists of a black band across the center of the shield with a central red spot flanked by a spot of blue gray on either side. A narrow circular band of red surrounded by black passes through the black band and encompasses the three spots and portions of the blue gray field that lies above and below the central band. Outside of this line is another band which is red on the upper two-thirds of the shield and yellow on the lower portion. In addition, the red portion indents toward the center of the shield on both sides of the dividing black band. The second design is rather simple, consisting of a yellow four-pointed star within an enclosing yellow band. The star has a central spot or circle of white, and it lies on a grayish white field. All the elements are outlined in black. The shield cover is of very nicely tanned buckskin decorated with a series of yellow spots that cover the entire outer surface in rows. In one portion of the cover is a very large hole that has been neatly mended. This hole looks as if it would align with the large hole in the shield but does not. A tear along the bottom of the cover has also been mended.

SANTA ANA SHIELD

FH 1605 CI   Figures 55 and 56

PURCHASED IN SANTA ANA prior to 1908, this shield is 21 inches in diameter and ¼-inch thick. It is composed of two thicknesses of leather held together by five rings of blind stitching and a rim binding. The peripheral stitching is a very even cobbler's stitch set in a slight groove. The margin of the shield is badly broken, possibly due to the extreme convexity of this particular specimen; however, all breaks have been mended. The central hand loop of buckskin thongs is still present although not tied. The neck sling is

FIGURE 55

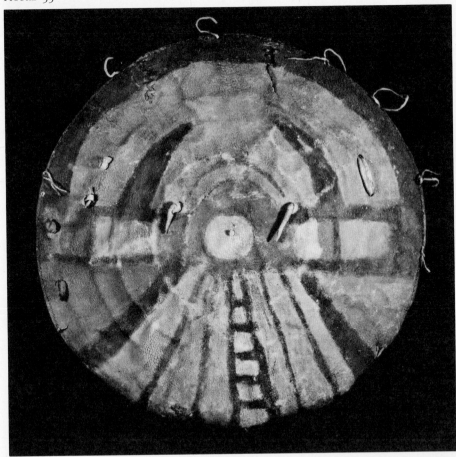

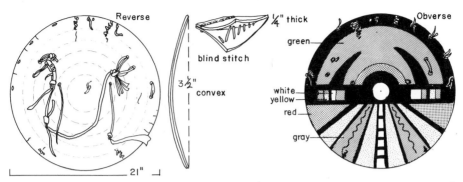

Reverse

green

white
yellow
red

gray

blind stitch

¼" thick

convex

3½"

21"

Obverse

FIGURE 56

attached to loops set in paired holes on either side of the shield well above the horizontal axis. The sling is of interest because it is riveted together on one side with buckskin knots. Hanging loop holes are present at the top of the shield although a break has destroyed one hole. Along the right-hand side of the shield at the horizontal axis is an additional loop. This loop is present on all Santa Ana shields and is of undetermined use. Peripheral decorative ties are present around the top two-thirds of the shield. These ties are buckskin thongs that have been stitched through the shield. A rather long buckskin decorative tie is present in the center of the shield. The design is a horizontal black band with rectangular insets of yellow, white and blue gray blocks at either side and a central spot of white. At either side of the band rise two black horns that almost meet in a field of blue green above the central band. Above the white circle, and more or less enclosed within these horns, lies an arc of red. The blue green field is surrounded by a black margin. Below the central band are a series of varicolored rays. At either side of the central band is a triangle of red with a black outlining stripe. Immediately next to these are broad yellow stripes, then narrow stripes of blue gray with wavy black lines in the center. Next are even broader stripes of yellow. Running from the central white circle to the bottom rim of the shield is a band of white that is broken with a black ladder design.

SANTA ANA SHIELD

FH 1619 CI   Figures 57, 58 and 59

THIS INTERESTING SHIELD was purchased in Santa Ana in 1907. It is composed of two pieces of hide ⅜ inch thick and held together by elaborate stitching. It has the appearance of having been bi-lobed at one time, but the bottom has been sheared off, cutting away part of the stitching and the bottom lobes. The manner of stitching is Spanish in that the leather thongs form a design on both the front and the back of the shield. The leather thongs on the front show a smaller portion of the stitches than they do on the reverse. The hand loop, if it is such, is completely atypical for it lies on the right-hand side of the shield at practically the horizontal axis. All other examples of Santa

FIGURE 57

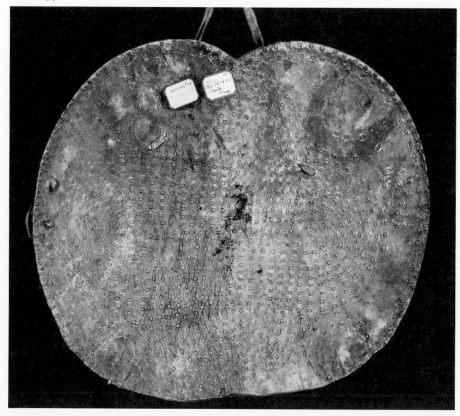

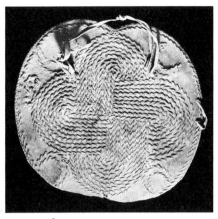

FIGURE 58

Ana shields have this loop in addition to the hand grip loop. The neck sling is attached by two sets of paired holes placed quite high on the shield, at least a third of the distance above the horizontal axis. The original decoration was a double line of stitching around the periphery of the shield. Occupying the center of this field is a filfot cross made with nine individual thongs. Within the notch or angle formed by each arm of the cross is a crescent done in stitches. Probably of Indian origin is the presence of a red smudge within the arms of each crescent moon which is itself a dark brown. The shield appears to be a Spanish soldier's, as it very closely fits the description of an *adarga*. Undoubtedly, an *adarga* came into the hands of a Pueblo Indian who decorated it and attempted to cut it in such a way that it would be round, but abandoned the effort after cutting away the bottom third of the stitching.

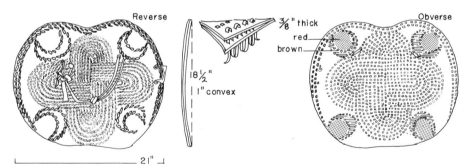

FIGURE 59

69

SANTO DOMINGO SHIELD

FH 1600 CI   Figures 60 and 61

THIS SHIELD, purchased at Santo Domingo around 1910, is 24 inches in diameter. It was made of two sheets of leather ⅜ inch thick stitched together with five rings of blind stitching and the edges joined with a cobbler's stitch. The shield is concave, but appears to have buckled into this shape through poor care. There is a large rip in the center of the shield that has been repaired with rawhide; however, portions of this stitching have worn out or been broken. Running diagonally across the rear of the shield are several long dark stains or splashes that, in one place, have gathered in a pool along the bottom rim of the shield. When tested, these stains were found to be blood. The central rear portion is worn smooth on both sides of the large break. The shield ties have been changed so that their positions are difficult to reconstruct. There are holes for the central hand loop placed along the horizontal axis and into the left-hand hole is inserted one of the neck sling straps. The support holes for the neck sling have been moved at least once leaving a set of six holes on either side and slightly above the horizontal axis of the shield. Attaching two loops in the left-hand holes to a single loop in the right-hand holes is a 32-inch strap. Tied to the single right hand loop is a small roll of cotton cloth about 1 inch in width that was either white or has lost all traces of color. There is a hanging loop at the top of the shield and onto this loop has been tied a portion of the right-hand strap of the neck sling. A few fragments of buckskin ties still remain around the edge of the shield. The exact center of the shield is perforated by a small hole probably for the addition of a decorative feather. Both the front and the back of this unusual shield have been decorated more than once. Based on the concavity of the shield plus the series of designs that have been over-painted, it has apparently been reversed. The first design on the present rear of the shield appears to have been a single black band across the shield. From the bottom of this single bar is suspended a line drawing of a circle with a pair of hands placed over the circle. The hands are drawn outstretched and extending from some type of material, at least the drawing conveys an impression of wrinkled sleeves. Following this design, the black bar was intensified and outlined with a series of dots. From the top of the line, a pair of inward-turned horns was added and three circles within the black band were added. The shield was then reversed and a new

70

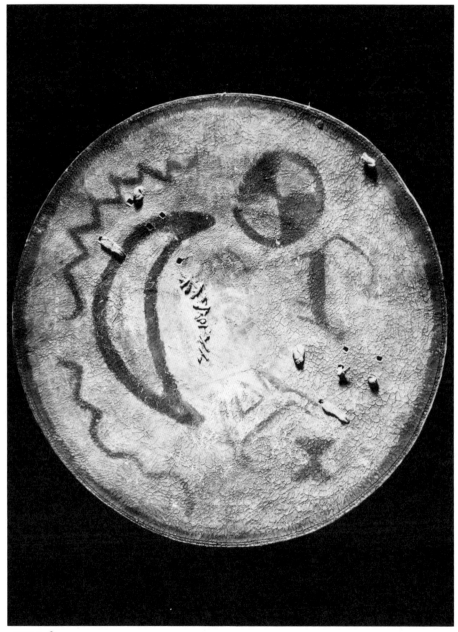

FIGURE 60

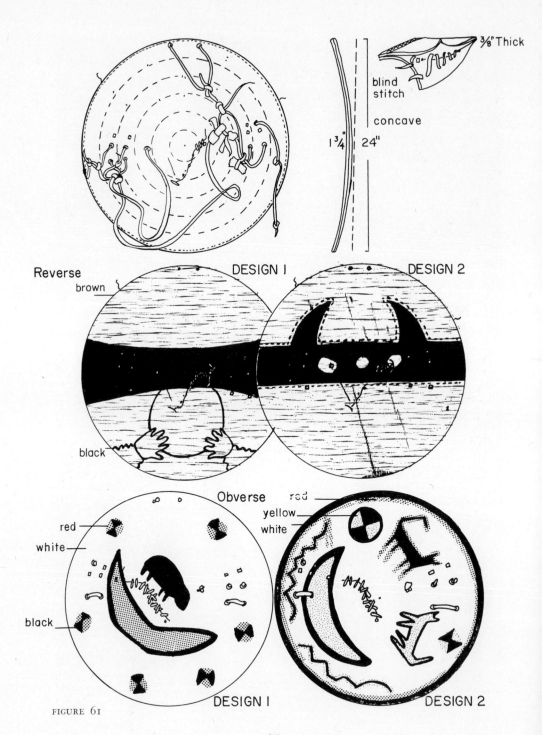

⅜" Thick

blind
stitch

concave

1¾"   24"

Reverse   DESIGN 1   DESIGN 2

brown

black

Obverse   red

red   yellow

white   white

black

DESIGN 1   DESIGN 2

FIGURE 61

set of designs appear in greater color. The first of these designs represents a red quarter moon with a black bear poised above it. Around them are six red circles within which are black hourglass figures. The entirety is placed on a white field. The final design is quite elaborate consisting of a black border within which is a narrow red stripe. On the left-hand side of the shield is a red and black water serpent and along the lower margin is a similar figure in yellow and black. Along the upper margin of the shield is a single yellow circle outlined in black with alternating quarters in black. A similar figure lies on the lower right-hand margin, but this figure does not have the black outlining and is slightly smaller than the upper one. Between these two designs are the figures of two animals. One done in black has a red outline and a slightly longer tail than its companion which is in yellow with a black outline. Both of these animals appear to represent Mountain Lions.

SANTO DOMINGO SHIELD

FH 1608 CI   Figures 62 and 63

THIS 22-INCH SHIELD was purchased in Santo Domingo in 1907. It is made of two pieces of leather ¼ inch thick, joined together by three concentric rings of blind stitching and a very neat cobbler's stitch at the rim. The outer rim of the shield has been broken and repaired in four places and a fifth split has been left unrepaired. All of the mending has been done with rawhide. The hand loop in the center of the shield appears to have been moved at

FIGURE 62

74

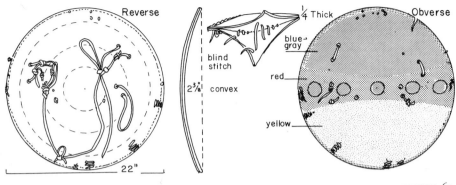

blind
stitch

2⅞ convex

¼ Thick

blue→
gray

red

yellow

Obverse

FIGURE 63

least once and the unwanted holes plugged with leather. Within an inch of
the left side hand loop hole that has been plugged lies another hole with the
remains of a strap in it. On the opposite or right side are two holes into which
a single thong has been inserted and knotted to make a loop. If this is the
hand loop, it is offside to both the neck sling and to the decoration on the
front of the shield. The neck sling consists of a two-hole attachment at either
side with a 24-inch leather thong joining them. There is a single small hole
in the center of the shield and again this probably represents a feather tie
attachment. A series of holes at the top of the shield indicate that it was hung
from the top margin, although no straps remain. However, only two of these
holes penetrate to the rear of the shield. The decoration on the front is a single
red bar across the horizontal axis of the shield within which are five circles of
blue gray color. The entire upper portion is blue gray also but rimmed by a
small red stripe. The lower portion is yellow with the same small stripe of red
at the margin of the shield.

SANTO DOMINGO SHIELD

FH 1613 CI   Figures 64 and 65

THERE IS NO PURCHASE DATE for this shield, but its appearance suggests it was made more recently than the others. The shield is 22½ inches in diameter and of a single ¼-inch thickness of hide from the neck of an animal. A central hand loop is present. The neck sling has a four-hole attachment with the straps broken out of the holes. On the left side only the upper left hole is still in use and on the right side, three of the holes are used, but none of the straps are still tied together. The neck strap that does join from the upper left side to the inside corner on the right is 30 inches in length. A hanging loop is present on the upper margin of the shield. Around the periphery is a strip of flannel which hangs 20 inches below the shield on either side leaving the bottom third bare. Both ends of the red cloth strip have two diamond-shaped openings and a half diamond cut into the cloth. Along the edges of the shield, the cloth has been tied in nine places and on some of these buckskin ties are remnants of what appear to be eagle feathers. The cloth is sewed in

FIGURE 64

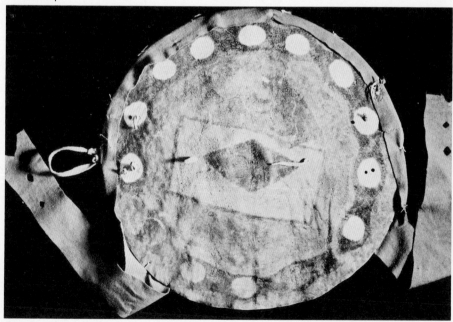

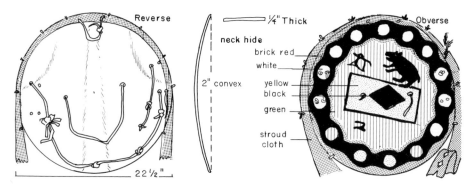

¼" Thick

neck hide

brick red

white

2" convex   yellow

black

green

stroud
cloth

Obverse

FIGURE 65

two places and tied in such a way that the cloth folds over the front and back surfaces of the shield. The decoration consists of a broad red band around the periphery of the shield enclosing a green field. Within the red band are ten white spots along the top and sides. Two yellow spots are along the base with a green spot at either side. These small circles of color are completely encircled in black with the red showing on either side of the black. The central green field shows a clear impression of ribbing as though the shield, while still damp, had been placed on a piece of corduroy cloth and weighted down. Within the green field on the upper half of the shield are a black bear and a bird-like form. The center of the shield has a yellow rectangle painted on it and surrounded by a black line. Centered within the rectangle is a black diamond shape. Below the rectangle is another figure in black that is unrecognizable.

SANDIA SHIELD AND COVER

FH 1596 CI   Figures 66, 67 and 68

PURCHASED IN SANDIA in 1912, the buyer noted that this shield was the
only one known to be in the pueblo for over ten years. The shield, 21 inches
in diameter, was made of a single 3/16-inch thickness of leather and was protected by a very thin buckskin or goatskin cover. The hip spots and the line of
the backbone show in the hide on the reverse side of the shield. To the left of
the vertical backbone line near the center is an area of heavy wear from use of
the hand grip. There are no breaks or mends in the shield. The hand loop
with a 6-inch opening still retains the thong knotted on the front as do all
other attachments. The neck sling had four attachment holes on either side
although only two are presently in use for the loops; the sling itself is missing.
No hanging loop is present although there is a series of holes around the
periphery and along the upper half of the center line of the shield. These
were undoubtedly used for the attachment of decorations. The painting of
this shield is quite complex but appears to have been re-done at least four
times. The first design was a simple series of concentric rings of color. The
rim had a narrow band of dark blue inside of which was a similar band of
red. Within this lay a broader band of gray blue around a large central white
spot. This was overlain in the second design by a blue green spot of copper
carbonate paint placed slightly above the horizontal axis and from which
radiate several elements. The bottom quarter was painted with five narrow
red stripes alternating with four broad white rays. The red paint appears to
be a hematite. At either side of this quadrant lay a wedge of blue green copper
carbonate paint as well as a centrally located one at the top of the shield.
Above the blue green wedges at either side was a broad white panel divided
by black lines into rays and surmounted by a field of blue black joining it to
the uppermost wedge. The third design was a single large yellow spot in the
center of the shield. The final design is a very elaborate black-and-yellow-
horned blue sun face on a white field that is flanked at either side in the bottom half by two blue-headed black-horned serpents. Directly above and below
the sun face lie three crosses or star symbols. The blue green sun face is haloed
by a band of black rays and an outer band of black hemispherical lobes. The
base of the black horns has been painted with a limonite paint. There is in
addition a faint indication of blue green and black in the upper right quad-

FIGURE 66

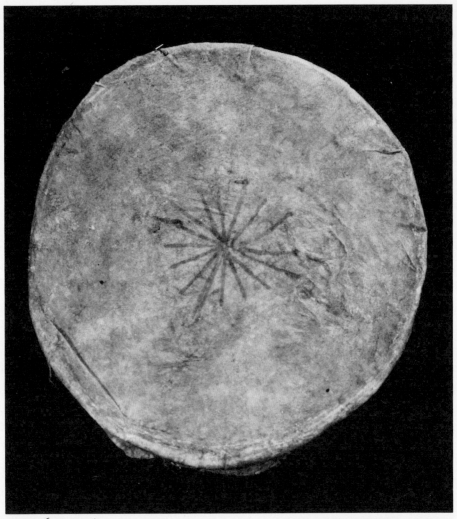

rant vaguely suggestive of another element, but too dim to identify. This re-
markable shield was protected by an extremely thin cover, probably of goatskin, with a badly smeared design in red, green and yellow. There appears to
have been a rayed element in red at the center and a green band at the edge.
Between these are a multitude of wiggly green and yellow lines and dots. The
general appearance of the shield is one of great age despite its excellent condition.

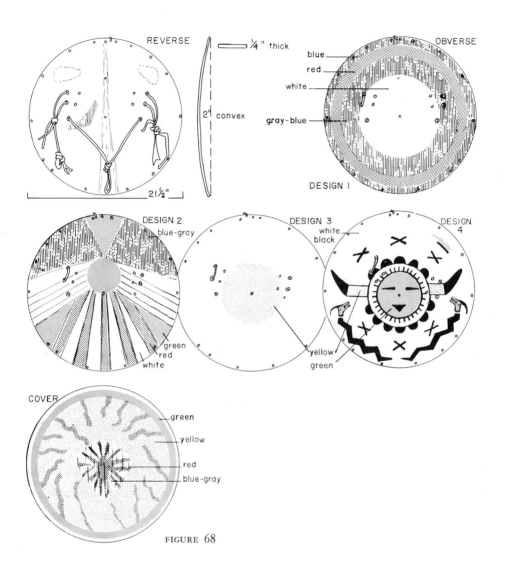

REVERSE

21/2"

1/4 " thick

2" convex

OBVERSE

blue
red
white
gray-blue

DESIGN 1

DESIGN 2
blue-gray

green
red
white

DESIGN 3
white
black

yellow
green

DESIGN 4

COVER

green
yellow
red
blue-gray

FIGURE 68

TAOS SHIELD AND COVER

FH 1598 CI   Figures 69, 70 and 71

PURCHASED IN TAOS in 1907, this 21-inch shield is made of the ¼-inch neck hide of some animal, probably a bullock, and is protected by a buckskin cover. There are three tears in the shield, one at the top and two at the bottom. All have been carefully mended with a rawhide thong. These tears may have resulted from the shield being forced from a concave to a convex position for now the shield is concave. Heavy wear shows on the back by the hand loop. The 6-inch-wide hand loop has been attached to the hanging loop, probably to keep it out of the way during recent years in storage. The attachments for the 30-inch neck sling have been moved many times as there are eight holes on either side. The method of attachment apparently involved two holes at a time with the loops being knotted at the rear of the shield. The thong used to mend the uppermost tear was left long probably for use as a hanging loop. There are no peripheral holes on the shield although a few bits of sinew remain in two or three places. Two designs are present on the shield. The first

FIGURE 69

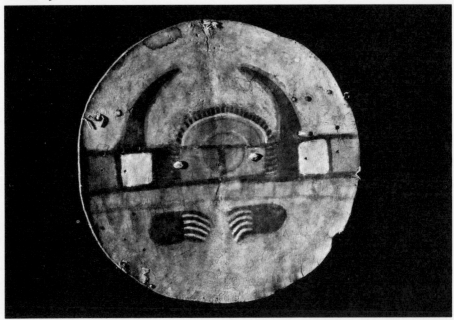

divided the shield in half horizontally by a black band. The band was broken in the center by a yellow hemisphere containing two black dots and a black circle. At either side of this element along the band were two rectangles and three spots, all in yellow. Overlying the band, the field was yellow while below it was blue gray. The second design retains the same blue gray lower field. The upper field is a much darker blue gray and is separated from the lower by a broad band of alternating red, white and black blocks with two black horn-like projections that rise from its upper margin. The band and the horns are outlined in red. Occupying the upper center of the band between the tips of the horns is a purplish spot ringed by white, then red, white again and then a rayed black design. In the lower field are two black bear tracks with toes pointing together and white painted between the toes. The cover of this shield is of buckskin that has been toned red over the entire exterior. Several small rents in the cover have been mended.

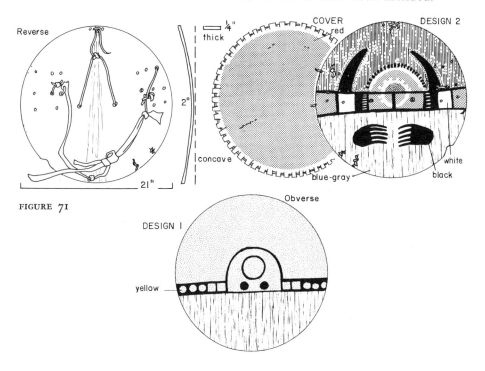

FIGURE 71

SPANISH SHIELD

FH 137 C, RH   Figures 72 and 73

UNFORTUNATELY, neither the provenience nor the purchase date for this eighteenth century Spanish officer's *adarga* is known. The dimensions of its bi-lobed form are 22 inches in width by 20½ inches in height. The shield is made of two ¼-inch hides with a ⅛-inch sheet of leather inserted between them. It is possible that the thinner piece was brought to the rear to cover the reverse side of the shield protecting the owner's hand and arm from the rough stitching. The hides are stitched together with a wide thong in a decorative filfot cross that shows on both sides. There are four places on the shield,

FIGURE 72

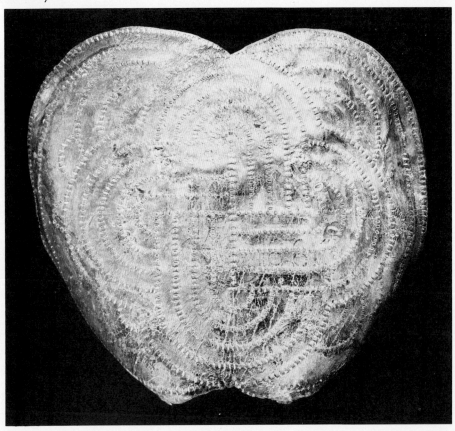

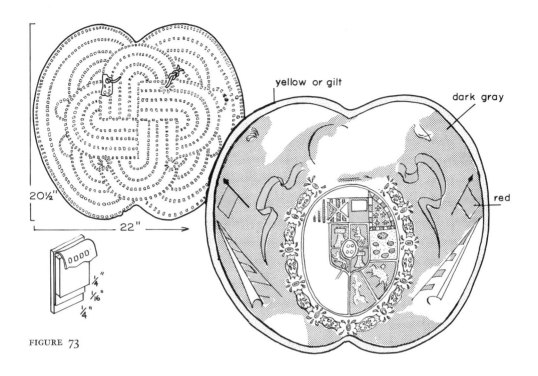

yellow or gilt

dark gray

red

20½"

22"

¼"

¹⁄₁₆"

¼"

FIGURE 73

one centered in each quadrant, that have been encircled by stitching. These may represent the earliest attachment of the hand or hand-and-arm grip of the *adarga*. However, all but the upper left strap have been sheared off. The left-hand fastening consists of a fragment of strap leather riveted to the shield with rawhide inserted through it. At the end of the leather strap is a buckskin thong inserted through it and knotted. The upper right-hand fastening is also a simple buckskin thong. On the left margin of the shield face are two perforations on the horizontal axis that have been punched through after the *adarga* was decorated. These holes and the buckskin ties undoubtedly represent native revamping of the *adarga*. The painted decoration of the shield is badly deteriorated, but enough fragments of gilt, black, and red paint remain to identify the Royal Spanish coat-of-arms at the center surrounded by several other elements that were not identified but undoubtedly represent family crests. This central element was surrounded by a dark gray field emblazoned with ensigns in red. The margin of the shield had been gilded. Separating this band from the field color was a single black line.

SPANISH SHIELD   FH 1537 CI   Figures 74 and 75

NEITHER PROVENIENCE NOR PURCHASE DATE is known for this *adarga* although its tag from the Fred Harvey Company refers to it as a "buffalo shield." The bi-lobed shield is 19 inches in width and 18½ inches in height and is made of three sheets of hide with a combined thickness of ⅝ inch. The three pieces of leather are stitched together by a broad thong of hide in the decorative form of a filfot cross that is visible on both sides. However, the reverse side of the shield was formerly covered by a thin sheet of leather which passed under the hand grip attachments and the marginal stitching, and was then inserted between the leather of the shield face and the back two

FIGURE 74

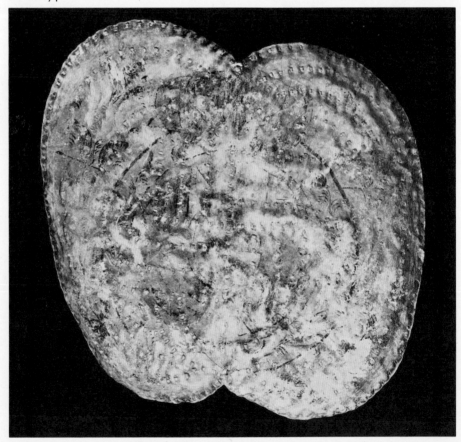

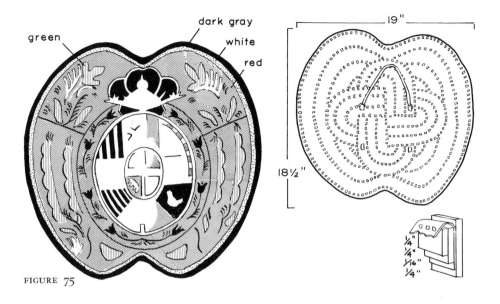

green · dark gray · white · red

19"

18½"

¼" ¼" ⅟₁₆" ¼"

FIGURE 75

pieces. Undoubtedly this served as a protection for hand and arm from the rough stitching. Fragments of this backing leather remain under some of the stitching and the hand grip attachments. The four attachments for the arm and hand grip of the *adarga* have been trimmed down to buttons, one in each quadrant of the shield. Fastened to the upper two by buckskin thongs is a heavy hide thong attached in the manner of native shields. The shield is painted with a central element that is undoubtedly a family crest encircled by a floral motif in black and gilt on red. Large additional floral motifs lie at either side of the central element and are painted in dark green and white on a red field. A stylized crown in black and gilt is placed above the central crest. The margin of the shield has been painted with a narrow band of white and outside of this a thin black band. The execution of this shield is much poorer in quality than FH 137 both in painting and in the construction, and may well represent a native product of the New Mexican Spanish.

IT IS APPARENT that shields were an artifact known to the Southwestern tribes long before the advent of the Spanish. The brief glimpses afforded by petroglyph and mural show the use of a round shield and we know from actual specimens that at least one group used round basketry shields between 1100–1300 A.D. The invading Spanish brought their own shield forms to the Southwest. One was the bi-lobed *adarga* used by the horsemen and the other the round metal *rodelo*. The latter was different in size, form, method of handling and presumably material from the *adarga,* and was used primarily by the foot soldier. If the native people borrowed an artifact it would be the form most familiar to them which in this instance would be the round shield of the Spanish foot soldier rather than the *adarga* of a mounted lancer. In either case the native or the Spanish traditions could have produced the round leather shields of the Pueblos that are represented in the Harvey Collection. It is most probable that the shields represent a melding of both traditions.

To make a good leather shield, however, requires not only a knowledge of leatherworking but a good source of hides. Prior to the coming of the Spanish the hides that were available to the Indians were primarily the rather thin skins of deer, elk, mountain sheep and mountain lion. If used for a shield these would require multiple layers to stop an arrow. While the thick skins of both buffalo and bear were available they do not appear to have been traditionally used. Bear skin in particular does not appear to have been used, either because of the difficulty in obtaining it or a taboo prohibiting its use. On the other hand bison hide is the right thickness but difficult to work with because of its green weight. With the advent of the Spanish, however, a new source of hides was introduced and inferentially new methods of working leather. The horse, mule, burro and bullock all had desirably heavy hides across both the hips and forequarters as well as the added attraction of being readily available when needed. The late Doc Williams of Flagstaff, a well-known saddlemaker and leatherworker for over sixty years, assisted in the identification of the leathers in the shields and the various methods of working the materials.

In the Harvey Collection the hides used in sixteen of the thirty shields are less than 3/16 inch thick. These have been doubled to make a shield of the desired thickness of 1/4 inch. Ten of the shields are of single hides that range between 1/4 and 3/8 inch in thickness. It would seem that the heavier hides were either not preferred or not as easily procured. The Spanish shields with multiple leathers are both over 1/2 inch thick while those that are of Spanish style: Acoma 1611 and 1620, Santa Ana 1619; are all over 1/4 inch in thickness. The use of leather thongs as a decorative element and the cobbler's stitch in an incised groove at the rim of the shield are undoubtedly of Spanish introduction. The hidden stitch used in attaching doubled hides appears to be a native contribution. It is far beyond the scope of this report to attempt a comparison of Indian and Spanish treatment of hides, but hides were for both native and Spaniard the most readily available material for manufacture or repair. Rawhide took the place of nails, wire and rope, leather was a universal covering and lacing material, buckskin was soft and decorative, and each undoubtedly had its acceptable niche.

Disregarding the uniquely shaped *adarga* of the Spanish and considering only the round shields in the collection it will be noted that there are three rather distinct techniques of working leather to produce a shield. Arbitrarily characterized, the first of these three is the Plains form. No attempt was made in this report to determine if this form had native roots or was an outgrowth of the Spanish horse-lance-shield complex. The shield is a single piece of heavy leather well-tanned but not hardened, which is either left plain or given the very simplest of designs. Decoration was lavished on the multiple covers. Attachments were usually of cloth and not buckskin or leather. The second technique is that of the Spanish, in which two or more sheets of leather were joined by decorative lacing thongs that are visible on both sides of the shield. Quite often the shield was backed with a thin soft leather or buckskin to protect hand and arm from the roughness of the lacings. Decorations were usually of family or the royal crest of Spain. The attachments are of leather and of a different style than those of the native shields. The Pueblo shield is the third type which utilized two forms. One is superficially similar to the Plains type, being a single piece of heavy leather. However, it is much larger in diameter and the leather is hardened. It is very similar to the Spanish *rodela* except that it is of hide rather than metal. Symbolic decoration is abundant on the shield and not on the single cover. Attachments are of buckskin or leather. The second Pueblo form joined two sheets of well-tanned leather by hidden stitching in the same technique used in making their moccasins. The leather was not usually hardened nor was it as thick as the first type. Again the shield, rather than the single cover, was elaborately decorated. Attachments were of buckskin or leather. It is possible that this was an adaptation of the body armor or *cuera* brought by the Spanish from Mexico. The *cuera* consisting of multiple layers of leather stitched together could effectively turn the ball of an *arquebus*.

The use of the shield differed also for the three groups. The Plains tribes used their shield primarily as a banner. It was an heraldic device that visibly showed they were protected from harm by the supernatural, and they did not need it to deflect actual physical attack. The shield was kept covered when in use as a banner and was actually bared only when fighting to avoid loss of its potency. The heraldic aspects of the Plains shield shares a certain similarity with the Spanish shield emblazoned with a royal crest or the heraldry of some proud family. The Spanish shield was an extension or attachment to the arm. The forearm was thrust through two leather loops with the hand grasping the last loop or a hold near the rim of the shield. It could then be easily maneuvered to turn or ward off blows. It did not, however, have the versatility of the Pueblo shield as a defensive armament. The Pueblo neck sling allowed the warrior to drop his shield and use both hands for a bow and arrows and yet retrieve it instantly, or use it with a single hand to parry a club blow, sling it across his back in an instant to protect his retreat. There is ample evidence of interchange between these groups such as the cutdown *adarga* from Santa Ana (1619) or the Spanish style decoration seen in the two shields from Acoma (1611 and 1620). Shields from Acoma (1618 and 1621) and Zia (1615) show incising on the back side, a technique reputed to be unique to the Apache. Some of the shields such as Acoma 1621, Zuñi 1595, and Santa Ana 1619 are much closer in diameter to Plains shields than they are to Pueblo.

The designs on the Pueblo shields were undoubtedly believed to be efficacious in enlisting the aid of the supernatural when in battle but they were also distinctive enough to have served as identity devices for the various tribes as well. Certainly Acoma's choice of circular designs differs radically from the horned elements preferred by Jemez. The Harvey Collection, however, does not have sufficient examples of all Pueblo groups to define these differences. The use of stylized stars, moons, and suns, and the realistic portrayal of animals of prey, are almost universal symbols of war throughout the Southwest, but the presence of the horned device of Jemez or the use of a water serpent, a germinative figure, on a war shield is not as easily explained.

One fact stands forth clearly, shields were important. They were kept covered and repainted as the designs dimmed or the shield passed into other hands. They were mended and reused even when they had sustained massive damage. The shields present a rather wide variety of battle damage. Acoma 1607 and Santa Ana 1605 have cuts that may have resulted from sword or lance thrusts on the surface of the shield. Acoma 1621 has a single bullet hole while Santa Ana 1603 has two. With the cooperation of Dr. Garland Wood of Flagstaff, an examination of the shields by xerography clearly showed compression rings around the perforations in these specimens indicating an impact velocity achieved only by a bullet. In all cases the leather fibers were driven toward the rear of the shield for a diameter almost double the actual size of the bullet hole. Arrows while more numerous were not as effective and none completely penetrated any of the shields examined. Acoma 1618 had three arrow cuts, Acoma 1621 two, Zia 1615 six, Jemez 1604 and 1612 one each. Breakage, another form of damage to the shields, is quite common. While it is possible to break the leather by warping the shield from convex to concave as appears to have been the custom when covering them, such a break occurs only along the periphery of the shield at roughly right angles to the margins. Other shields using double leathers blind stitched together occasionally show a curved breakage following the lines of stitching as in Jemez 1616. Rents believed to be club incurred are sharply angled breaks and occur more toward the center of the shield such as in Acoma 1614 with one break, Acoma 1618 one, Acoma 1610 two, Santo Domingo 1600 one, and Zia 1615 one. The break in Acoma 1614 is visible only on the backing leather of the shield. In addition to these evidences of use several of the shields have dark stains on their surfaces (Santo Domingo 1617 and 1600, Jemez 1604). These stains when tested by Wm. Hamilton, medical technician, were found to be blood stains.

Dr. Garland Wood when investigating the designs on the shields to determine if they could be separated by xerography pointed out that while the designs were not separable the resultant pictures did indicate mineral and vegetal paints. Vegetal paint used for black, yellow, blue and red did not photograph while the mineral paints for a dark yellow, red, blue green and white showed clearly.

It is probably not accurate to assume that each warrior carried a shield, for indications are that shields were costly to make and that in certain groups such as the Apache, only individuals with great personal power carried them. That they were of great value is indicated by their preservation until 1900 A.D. when the Harvey shields were collected. A survey of leading museums and individual collectors has yielded less than 150 specimens in the United States and a mere dozen in Europe with the Harvey Collection being the largest.

The question of how old the shields are is very difficult to answer even partially. Most were venerable when they were collected at the turn of the century and represented many times the only surviving specimens in their individual pueblos. The need for shields had virtually ceased for the Pueblo people of the Rio Grande with the increasing efforts of the United States Government forces against marauding tribes. The Rio Grande had been cleared as far south as Socorro by mid-century. With the cessation of raids the manufacture of shields should also have ceased. An examination of the shields indicates that many showing the most extensive hand and arm wear such as Jemez 1609, Sandia 1596, and Santo Domingo 1600, are examples of excellent workmanship. Others that are less worn and in better overall condition are not as well made while still others appear to have been made after the craft had fallen into disuse. Tesuque 1623 follows the traditional method of manufacture so poorly that it is difficult to believe that the maker had ever seen a shield. The presence of flags on the laterals of the *adarga* such as Spanish 137 was first introduced in 1725. By 1772 every presidio soldier was required to have a shield but by 1825 shields were being phased out because of the introduction of more powerful guns (Brinkerhoff: 1965: 21). The inference that is drawn from these scattered data is that probably the majority of the shields, whether native or Spanish, were used between 1700 and 1850 A.D. with one or two being made as late as the period from 1850 to 1900 A.D.

The Harvey Collection is without doubt the best and the largest representation of this little-known facet of Pueblo life.

BANCROFT, H. H. *History of Arizona and New Mexico, in Works,* Vol. XVII. San Francisco, 1889.

BOLTON, HERBERT EUGENE. *Kino's Historical Memoir of Pimeria Alta,* 2 vol. 2d ed. Berkeley, University of California Press, 1948.

BOURKE, JOHN G. *The Snake-Dance of the Moquis of Arizona.* London: Sampson Low, Marston, Searle & Rivington, 1884.

BRINKERHOFF, SIDNEY B., and ODIE B. FAULK. *Lancers for the King.* Arizona Historical Foundation. Phoenix, Arizona, 1965.

CUSHING, FRANK HAMILTON. *Outlines of Zuñi Creation Myths.* 13th Annual Report, Bureau of American Ethnology, Washington, D.C., 1891–92

DANIELS, HELEN SLOAN. *The Ute Indians of Southwestern Colorado.* Durango Public Library Museum Project, National Youth Administration. Durango, Colorado, 1941.

EZELL, PAUL H. *The Hispanic Acculturation of the Gila River Pimas.* American Anthropological Association. Vol. 63, No. 5, Part 2, Memoir 90, 1961.

FORDE, C. DARRYL. *Ethnography of the Yuman Indians.* University of California publication in American Archaeology and Ethnology. Vol. 28, 1931.

Franciscan Fathers, The. *An Ethnologic Dictionary of the Navajo Language.* St. Michaels, Arizona, 1910.

GOODWIN, GRENVILLE. *Western Apache Raiding and Warfare.* Edited by Keith H. Basso. Tucson: The University of Arizona Press, 1971.

HOTZ, GOTTFRIED. *Indian Skin Paintings from the American Southwest.* University of Oklahoma Press, Norman, 1970.

JUDD, NEIL M. Smithsonian Miscellaneous Collection. Vol. 124, 1954.

KROEBER, A. L. *Walapai Ethnography.* American Anthropological Association Memoir No. 42, 1935.

KLUCKHOHN, CLYDE and W. W. HILL and LUCY WALES KLUCKHOHN. *Navaho Material Culture.* The Balknap Press of Harvard University Press, Cambridge, Massachusetts, 1971.

MORRIS, EARL H. *Burials in the Aztec Ruin and the Aztec Ruin Annex.* American Museum of Natural History Anthropological Papers, Vol. XXVI, Parts III and IV, New York, 1924.

MORRIS, EARL H. and ROBERT F. BURGH. *Anasazi Basketry*. Basketmaker II through Pueblo III. A study based on specimens from the San Juan River Country. Carnegie Institution of Washington, Publication 533, 1941.

MORSS, NOEL. *The Ancient Culture of the Fremont River in Utah*. Papers of the Peabody Museum of American Archaeology and Ethnology, Harvard University. Vol. XII, No. 3, 1928–29, Cambridge, 1931.

MOONEY, JAMES. *Work in Esthetology*. Bureau of American Ethnology. 23rd Annual Report. Washington, 1904.

MUENCH, DAVID and DONALD G. PIKE. *Anasazi: Ancient People of the Rock*. American West Publishing Company, Palo Alto, California, 1974.

OPLER, MORRIS E. *An Apache Life-Way*. The Economic, Social and Religious Institutions of the Chiricahua Indians, University of Chicago Press, Chicago, 1941.

PARSONS, ELSIE CLEWS. *Hopi Journal of Alexander M. Stephen*. Columbia University Contributions to Anthropoolgy, Vol. 23, New York, 1936.

POWELL, JOHN WESLEY. *Anthropology of the Numa*. Smithsonian Contributions to Anthropology, No. 14, Washington, D.C., Smithsonian Press, 1971.

RUSSELL, FRANK. *The Pima Indians*. Bureau of American Ethnology. 26th Annual Report. Washington, 1908.

SMITH, WATSON. *Kiva Mural Decorations at Awatovi and Kawaika-a*. Reports of the Awatovi Expedition, No. 5. Papers of the Peabody Museum of American Archaeology and Ethnology, Harvard University, Vol. XXXVII. Cambridge, Massachusetts, 1952.

SPIER, LESLIE. *Havasupai Ethnography*. Anthropological Papers of the Museum of Natural History. Vol. XXIX. 1928.

STEVENSON, MATILDA COXE. *The Zuñi Indians*. 23rd Annual Report. Washington, 1904.

TITIEV, MISCHA and WILSON D. WALLIS. *Hopi Notes from Chimopovy*. Michigan Academy of Science, Arts, and Letters, Papers, Vol. 30, pt. 4, pp. 523–55.

TREUTLEIN, THEODORE E. *Pfefferkorn's Description of the Province of Sonora*. Albuquerque, University of New Mexico Press, 1949.

UNDERHILL, RUTH. *Here Come the Navajo*. A history of the largest Indian Tribe in the United States: Bureau of Indian Affairs, Publication Service, Haskell Institute, Lawrence, Kansas, 1953.

WOODARD, ARTHUR. *The Pima*. Masterkey Vol. VII, No. 6, November 1933.